The Galts:
A Canadian
Odyssey

H. B. Timothy

The Galts:
A Canadian
Odyssey

John Galt 1779-1839

McClelland and Stewart

McClelland and Stewart Limited,
The Canadian Publishers,
25 Hollinger Road,
Toronto, Ontario.
M4B 3G2

Design: Michael van Elsen

Printed and Bound in Canada.

Contents

To
the memory of
Henry Gordon Harvey Smith

Preface

In answer to the question put to me when I set out to write this book, "Where does the story begin?", I remember saying, "In Irvine, the birthplace of John Galt." I might, on reflection, now be more inclined to say that the story begins in Canada, and, to be more precise, in the churchyard of the Mohawk Chapel, in Brantford, Ontario. There, in an unmarked grave close to the tomb of Joseph Brant, the Mohawk chief, rest the remains of William Gilkison who founded the Elora settlement beside the tributary of the Grand River, which he himself named the "Irvine." We have to hear, first of all, why Gilkison chose that name.

In the vicinity of Loudon Hill bordering on John Galt's native Ayrshire, Scotland, the Irvine River rises and, as it gathers volume, makes its way down the valley, through the busy town of Kilmarnock where there were relatives of Galt. Westward of Kilmarnock, the river skirts the village of Dreghorn, the "Dalmailing" of Galt's *Annals of the Parish,* where he also had relatives. A few miles further on, it enters Irvine, passing quite close at one point to the house where he was born, and, at no great distance from it, flows into the Firth of Clyde. It was after this river that Gilkison named the tributary of the Grand, for he, too, was born in Irvine, in 1777.

Galt tells us that "the most remote idea of becoming connected" with Canada "never occurred" to him, though various circumstances from time to time reminded him of it. "Among others," he remarks,

a relation, a schoolfellow, went out to that country when young, and by him, as we sometimes corresponded, the province was kept in mind; – he came to London, and staying with me I picked out of him all the information I could, respecting Upper Canada;[1] the particulars were afterwards embodied in a paper, which professed to be a

7

statistical account of the country, and was published in the *Philosophical Magazine*.[2]

The relation and schoolfellow referred to was William Gilkison. In a footnote to the above observations on this subject, Galt, alluding to the news of Gilkison's death having reached him the day before, says: "he returned to Upper Canada where he bought half a township to settle on my plan." He also says in reference to the Gilkison connection:

As a member of the Society for the Encouragement of Arts, I exerted myself to induce the Committee of the proper department to offer a medal or premium for the cultivation of hemp in that country [Upper Canada] and the endeavour was successful; but I know not the effect, only I observed in the Gazette, when I first went to the province, an advertisement, which reminded me of the circumstance. Mr. Gilkison, at my instigation, obtained by the late Earl of Selkirk, in the tenders for hemp, Canadian hemp to be inserted; but still the notion of taking any particular interest in that region never was then conceived by me; – the country became however, more circumstantially known.

This incident is, in itself, not deserving of notice, but as a link in an important chain it merits serious attention; few biographical sketches with which I am acquainted, present, indeed, such a series of transactions, that so well deserve the epithet of fatal, in the philosophical sense of the term.[3]

John Galt is known, if he is known at all in Canada, as the founder of the Canada Company. Some years ago an editorial appeared in the Canadian press, the main part of which reads as follows:

Going – going – gone

The Canada Company is to disappear this month. Formed in 1824 it helped to settle about 2.5 million acres of Ontario land on the east of Lake Huron.

Now all the land is gone in the tract from Galt to Goderich. But the old marks of settlement remain: There is secretary John Galt's spokes-of-a-wheel-plan for Guelph and Goderich – and for tiny Bayfield which forgot to grow. There's the twist in the old Huron Road at Punkeydoodle's Corners where the surveyors changed course to hit Goderich – and crossed a river at a ford a few miles west to found Stratford.

There are the stone houses and the soft brick of early days, the carriage stops, the old Canada Co. office at Goderich, and the nearly

100-year-old Goderich court house, now slated for destruction.

Canada, west of Montreal, is a very young land, built by men who died only yesterday. It may be another hundred years before people realize that treasures from the past should be honoured.[4]

Galt wrote in *The Literary Life* that although it could not be said that he had in his own person accomplished much, he had sown the seeds of things that in the course of nature might attain magnitude and afford shelter. With something of this in mind a writer has said of him: "He adds another to the long list of his countrymen who have gone forth to sow what other men gather into barns."[5]

This book sets out to tell the story of how and where the seed was sown, and of the harvest it has yielded through the years across the changing vistas and the vastness of this land, whose dominion, in large measure due to the labours of John Galt and his immediate descendants, now extends "from sea to sea."

Neither in this volume, nor in the one to follow, however, will any attempt be made to provide a definitive biography of John Galt or of those who succeeded him in the great enterprise which began with him in Canada. In a study which undertakes to span three generations the definitive biography approach would result in a book of inordinate length from both the publisher's and the reader's point of view. Attention will be focused mainly on the achievements of the Galts dealt with, as makers of Canada. "The book which will do justice to this distinguished family and their collective pioneering activities has still to be written," wrote Jennie W. Aberdein.[6] The present work is offered as a modest contribution to that end.

To the following present-day descendants of John Galt whose sustained interest in the writing of this book has proved most encouraging, as well as to other individuals not related to the Galts, the author wishes to express his gratitude: Mrs. T. Galt, Atlantic Beach, Florida; the late A. T. Galt Durnford, the late E. A. Durnford, and Amy Durnford, Montreal; the late Arthur Galt, and Mrs. Galt, Barrhill, Ayrshire, Scotland; Mrs. Mary Galt, Toronto; Mr. and Mrs. T. B. Heney, Montreal; Mr. L. H. G. Kortright, and Mrs. Kortright, Snr., Toronto; Mr. G. B. Moser, Kendal, Westmorland, England; the late Miss A. Savage, Montreal; Mrs. C. Smith, Winnipeg; Mr. and Mrs. H. Turner, Winnipeg; Mrs. M. Wilson, Goderich, Ontario; Dr. J. W. Aberdein, Aberdeen, Scotland; and the late Mr. William Ross of the *Herald,* Irvine, Ayrshire, Scotland. For the gift of family records and much research material I owe the late H. G. H. Smith of Winnipeg a debt of gratitude I never could repay.

Dr. Aberdein generously gave me all the material she collected for her excellent study of John Galt, published by the Oxford University Press in 1936, and including copies of the letters that passed between the Directors of the Canada Company in London and John Galt as well as others involved in the work of the Company; of Galt's letters to William Blackwood, the Edinburgh publisher; and of Galt's correspondence with J. G. Lockhart. Mrs. Mary Galt of Toronto kindly loaned me the originals of Elizabeth Galt's letters, also copies of John Galt's letters to Dr. David Macbeth Moir. Generous use has been made of all these letters in the first volume of this work but there seemed no need to footnote each mention of any of them in the text, since the sources are given here. Galt's *Autobiography* has been used quite extensively. It is carrying prejudice against Galt a little too far, one feels, to suggest that his *Autobiography* is the work of an embittered man.[7] There is a great deal in it, even in that part of it which deals with his work in Canada, which is quite devoid of the gall of bitterness.

I also wish to thank Mr. D. W. H. Neilson of Catton Hall, Barton-Under-Needwood, Staffordshire, England, for giving me permission to obtain photocopies of the Wilmot Horton papers, known as the Catton Collection, in the custody of Derbyshire County Library, and others whom there is not room here to name for various ways in which they have assisted me.

These acknowledgements, however, would not be quite complete without a special word of thanks to Mr. J. G. McClelland of McClelland and Stewart Limited, Toronto, who listened to the story I had to tell and considered it worth publishing.

The Galts:
A Canadian
Odyssey

Chapter 1

SCOTTISH HERITAGE

Present-day descendants of John Galt in Canada have claimed that the family is of Danish origin. If so, the Galts must have found their way to Scotland in the wake of the Norse invaders who once harried the Western Isles and the adjoining coastal areas, being latterly settled mainly in the Irvine, Dreghorn and Stewarton parts of Ayrshire. John Galt himself asserted in his *Literary Life and Miscellanies* that, according to tradition, his Scottish forbears "with some of the Stuarts got hold of the lands of Stuarton, or Stewarton," and that they migrated there from Perthshire where they were originally located. The opening words of a book he began to write, but never finished, read as follows:

> I have ever thought that the spirit by which the Scottish Covenanters[1] were actuated was one of the highest manifestations of a determination to maintain the rights of the people that has yet irradiated the history of mankind . . .
>
> Possibly I may be allowed to feel not quite disinterestedly respecting the exercise of the divine right of resistance by the Covenanters. I had two collateral ancestors engaged in proclaiming it.[2]

The two collateral ancestors referred to were John Galt of Gateside, and William Galt of the Waukmiln (Waukmill) of Wark (or Fairlie Crivoch), in the parish of Stewarton, who were not only engaged in proclaiming the divine right of resistance, but, by the 1684 proclamation of Charles II, were proscribed for doing so. John of Gateside was banished to Carolina in 1684 for refusing to declare the armed resistance of the Covenanters to episcopacy a rebellion.

Stewarton has from early times been famous for the making of Scotch bonnets (the "Tam o' Shanters" much worn in Galt's day). These bonnets were hand-knitted from home-grown wool, milled for the purpose of "wauking" or shrinking them, then dyed, the favourite colour being blue with indigo. Hence the name "dyster" applied to a person employed in the highly skilled finishing processes of the trade. In the grounds of Montgreenan House which lie partly in Stewarton parish are the remains of a waukmill. It was here that John Galt's grandfather, also named John Galt, lived and worked like his Stewarton forbears as a dyster; and it was here that his seafaring father, Captain John Galt was born in November 1750.

Irvine, a few miles southwest of Montgreenan, was, in the mid-eighteenth century, one of Scotland's leading seaports. The town had about it a strong maritime flavour. Sailors comprised a large proportion of the population and there were usually a good many sea captains living there. One local minister at the time of his installation is said to have remarked that he had not realized that so many of his congregation were "afloat." Some of the town's wealthiest inhabitants were those whose imposing places of residence proclaimed the rewards awaiting anyone who cared to go, as they had gone in youth, to try their fortune as planters in the West Indies and Jamaica. John Galt refers to children of such people working as planters in the East Indies, who in his boyhood were living and attending school at Irvine.

Galt's name and that of his birthplace are connected with an event which helped to make both maritime and Canadian history. On June 1, 1819, the *Jean,* a square sterned carvel built brigantine with one deck and two masts, sailed on her maiden voyage from Greenock. This famous vessel, which in her time held the record for the fastest crossing from the Clyde coast to Quebec and was for several years one of the main connecting links between Britain and the Canadas, was built at the Irvine shipyard by Gilkison, Thomson and Company. The Gilkison member of the firm; James Gilkison shipmaster of Irvine, who was one of the vessel's owners; and her captain, Alexander Allan of Saltcoats in the parish of Ardrossan, were all relatives of John Galt. When Galt was opening up the Huron Tract in Upper Canada, a large proportion of the passengers carried by the *Jean* were emigrants intending to settle there. She was the first of the famous Allan Line, later amalgamated with the Canadian Pacific Railway Company to form the Canadian Pacific fleet.

Irvine had a tolerably good school of seamanship, run by David Sillar who was schoolmaster, magistrate, poet and instructor in navigation all rolled into one. Sillar was the "dainty Davie" well beloved and immortalized by Scotland's national poet, Robert Burns. It would probably be at Sillar's school for seamen that John Galt's father qualified as master mar-

14

iner, having already, as required of candidates seeking admission to the course for the master's ticket, attained the rank of mate, then equivalent to first officer aboard a merchantman. His elevation to the mastermarinership immediately gave him a special status in a predominantly seafaring community such as Irvine was in those days. For example, at public worship in the ancient parish church, not only had the sailors a loft all to themselves compared with the other crafts or incorporated trades who had to share one loft among them but, in the sailors' loft there was a fine cushioned pew specially reserved for the shipmasters.

A half-length portrait in oils of Captain Galt showed him wearing a powdered wig and the colourful merchant marine uniform of his day. When he sat for the portrait he was holding in the crook of his right arm a brass telescope engraved with his name at the wide end, around the rim.[3] Fair-complexioned, good-looking, and over six feet tall, he must have cut an impressive figure as he walked through the streets of Irvine. There he was held in high esteem for his honesty and his unpretentious, good-natured disposition. At a public ceremony in Irvine on September 7, 1825 John Galt (the novelist) was made a burgess. Magistrate Fullarton who served him as a model for Mr. Pawkie in *The Provost,* on delivering the congratulatory address said in his markedly Highland accent that he had been well acquainted with Mr. Galt's father and that he was a "very decent man." The freedom of the royal and ancient burgh thus conferred on Galt might well have been in recognition of his forbears' long and prominent connection with the place, as well as for his own accomplishments. An Adam Galt is referred to in the town records as early as 1542. In 1608 another Adam Galt (possibly the same as Adam Galt, merchant burgess, 1612), was burgh treasurer. The town records for 1611 – 1665 show William Galt, mariner and burgess; William Galt, councillor; and Thomas Galt, collector. The latter may have been the Thomas Galt elected procurator fiscal in 1667. James Galt, smith, was made a burgess that same year, and, it would seem, was appointed by the town council to "dress the town Knock" (Clock) in the belfry beneath the Tolbooth steeple, and each day except Sunday to ring the bell in the morning, when the ports or town gates were opened, and at curfew, according to ancient custom. There is also mention of the sub-leasing to James Galt sometime after 1645 of the Howe or Holme or Hair Mill (one of the burgh mills for grinding corn or other grain), and of a John Galt, merchant, and a William Galt, skipper, in 1732, while from 1743 – 1745, a James Galt was apparently burgh mason, for his name occurs in connection with the procuring of building materials for work done on the prison (which was located in the Tolbooth), the bell-house and the school.

The house on the west side of the High Street to which Captain Galt brought his Greenock bride, Jean Thomson, in 1776 was "a very commonplace three-storey tenement." It was also at that time a veritable Galt colony for it was owned and occupied by relatives of Captain Galt, all more or less identified with the interests and activities of the local seafaring community. John Galt's birth on May 2, 1779 in the middle flat of the tenement, which his parents occupied, was followed by that of his sister, Agnes, on October 14, 1781, and of his two brothers, James and Thomas, on July 5, 1783 and April 19, 1785 respectively. The sister who outlived all the others was to play an important part in salvaging what was left of the wreckage of her eldest brother's fortunes in the closing years of his life. James died at Montego Bay, Jamaica, when only fifteen, and Thomas in Honduras when he was twenty-six years of age.

One is given little help in attempting to reconstruct Galt's early childhood from his random recollections on the subject in the *Autobiography*. He had, he tells us, a "singular local," but not a very good "general" memory,[4] though certain things stood out vividly through the years, the picture of Niagara Falls, for instance, which he saw briefly on a visit to the home of his relatives in the nearby town of Kilmarnock, and by which, he said, his "juvenile imagination was awfully excited." Nothing had ever produced such an effect on him nor could he conceive "anything more wild and wonderful than that view." When at the Falls many years later, he fancied himself "on the very spot below the town of Manchester on the American side from which the drawing had been taken."[5] As he looked back on the effect produced on him by the picture, it struck him "as one of those agitating and forcible impulses of destiny, which direct some men on in their course, and to the issue of their fortunes"; and subsequent events seemed to justify his regarding it "as belonging to the concatenations of Fate,"[6] the influence of which on human affairs he believed in all his life.

As influential was his strangely soul-stirring, almost ecstatic sort of encounter with the Buchanites, an apocalyptically-minded religious sect which had made its appearance in Irvine, but whose theological extravagances created such a stir that the magistrates ordered them out of the town. John was trotting alongside them as they marched out on the way, as they believed, to the New Jerusalem, with their chief instigator, Mrs. (Lucky) Buchan, daughter of a Banffshire tavernkeeper at their head, when his mother caught up with the procession and unceremoniously lugged him home. "I have not," he comments on the incident, "the slightest recollection of Mrs. Buchan's heresies – how could I? – but the scene and more than once the enthusiasm of the psalm singing has risen on my remembrance, especially in describing the convenanters in *Ringan Gilhaize.*"[7] There were other things of which he had vivid recollections but which he did not think readers of the *Autobiography* would care to hear about, since they featured in his novels.

He was always extremely reluctant to "broach domestic matters." The family side of his life in the Irvine period is consequently almost entirely hid from view. How he felt about his parents is, however, pretty clearly indicated in what follows:

> My father was one of the best, as he was one of the handsomest of men, but he was of an easy nature, with only passable ability, in which however probity was prominent. My mother was however a very singular person; possessing a masculine strength of character, with great natural humour, and a keen perception of the ridiculous in others. In her prime, as I would call it, she indulged in queer metaphorical expressions, exceedingly forcible and original. In latter life this grew so much into a habit, that her talk to strangers must have seemed often fantastical. The rich ore of her common sense, however, which pervaded her observations was always remarkable, and frequently extorted an instantaneous assent to her opinions while they provoked irrepressible laughter.[8]

With reference to his mother Galt related in the *Autobiography* an incident that occurred at a later period of his life. On a trip to Albany he met a Colonel Hamilton, son of Alexander Hamilton, one of the founding fathers of the United States of America. In consequence of this meeting Galt received an invitation to dine with the celebrated De Witt Clinton, governor of New York State. Galt found Mrs. Clinton to be "a woman of great energy, with many original traits of character." What particularly claimed his attention and called forth his respect was that in appearance she much resembled his mother. She was dressed in exactly the same style, and the resemblance was increased by the same straightforward shrewdness as his mother exhibited. Nothing, however, occurred to show that Mrs. Clinton possessed the same gift of humour, or the grotesque sort of phraseology which in his mother was almost equal to wit. Mrs. Clinton was a shade graver. The cordial treatment Galt received was due to the impression made on her by reading his *Annals of the Parish.*[9] E. W. Spaulding's biography of George Clinton has a portrait in profile of De Witt Clinton's wife, but her face was almost hidden by the head-dress she wore when the likeness was taken. What a pity that the portrait of Galt's mother, which the family prevailed on her to sit for, came to such a sorry end. When the picture was finished and shown to her she reacted by poking a hole in it![10]

Irvine, the cultural capital at one time of the west of Scotland, was in Galt's day widely known as a centre of education, its schools, as he noted, being "particularly good." Foremost among the latter was the Grammar School or the Latin School which was established in the middle of the sixteenth century by an endowment provided by Mary Queen of Scots. The schoolhouse, as reconstructed in 1750, consisted of an oblong, one-storey building, surmounted by a bell-turret, and with an entrance vestibule dividing it into two compartments, the English master occupying the one, and the Classics master the other. The school stood, with its playground surrounded by a wall, close up to and on the right hand side of the gate leading to the churchyard. At a later period the rector sometimes had more than twenty boarders. Boys from the West Indies and from America, before the War of Independence, were sent to Irvine to attend the Grammar School, at which Galt also received part of his education.

From time to time the name of Harriet Pigott crops up in these pages. When she was gathering material for an intended biography of Galt,[11] information about him was provided by two of his schoolfellows, G. J. Weir and Alexander Rodger. Weir wrote from Annan in the south of Scotland conveying what follows to Rodger for transmission to Miss Pigott:

> I shall now try from day to day to furnish all I know, directly, or indirectly, of Mr. Galt leaving you and the lady to extract from it what you may think proper . . .
>
> My first knowledge of Mr. Galt was . . . when he came to Irvine School to learn Latin, but the year having commenced six weeks, precisely, for beginners he was put to a desk by himself to overtake the others. But whether it was a love of play, or the novelty of things or that nature was strongly engaged with his body, (for tho he was said to be only 7 years of age, he was as big as a boy of 14) he was supposed incapable of overtaking the junior class after a month's trial and taken from the school. In my opinion a most unfortunate decision for him, as it prevented him, forever, from being a scholar, and this deficiency may have molested him in after life exceedingly; the best proof I have for this is, that Mr. Galt mentioned to me that he was determined his sons should be good scholars, and not [have] a smattering of learning only as he had.[12]

Weir's third guess at the reason for Galt's inability to catch up with the junior class at school – "that nature was strongly engaged with his body"

– accords with the explanation provided by Galt himself: "owing to my growth and consequent ailment I made comparatively little progress in my education, but," he adds, "I had a very clear idea of what I did learn, and never afterwards forgot it. Among other expedients to counteract my infirmity was being sent in the evening privately to take lessons in reading from the schoolmaster. In this task, which was desultorily executed, I read with him the Spectator and Gil Blas, and as I have never read either since, I am led to conclude that in these conclave instructions I evinced something of intelligence: when I left him" – when exactly Galt does not say – "he made me a present of Goldsmith's Roman History."[13]

According to Rodger, Galt's schoolmates

accounted him rather a dull boy in his earlier years. He was, for the most part, very awkward at all of the school-yard games: – it was probably by this however that they estimated him, at the same time not appreciating the more plodding disposition on his part, which most likely led him to estrange himself somewhat from them.[14]

A professed authority on Galt once wrote less sympathetically:

If he had enjoyed the rough and tumble of the playground what a difference it might have made on his relationships with men. If his nose had been bled a few times, or his shins kicked at football; if he had learned to play a losing game against impossible odds, and leave the field with head all bloody but unbowed. What a discipline he missed. Some of his vanity might have been knocked out of him and his singularity of temperament rubbed off.[15]

On the other hand, the modern educational psychologist would shudder at the thought of putting a beginner, late in starting school, at a desk by himself to catch up with the rest of the class. Galt's bigness for his age was bound to make him feel clumsy and awkward. It was, he explained, his "infirm state" that led him not only to avoid the healthy exercises of other boys, but to seek indoor amusement. That, too, probably explains his late arrival for enrolment in the Grammar School.

The extracurricular activities of the school were not designed to make it particularly attractive. On Sundays, the scholars occupied a special seat in the north aisle of the parish church, under the master's watchful eye. Following the first "diet" of public worship they were marched back to the school, examined closely on the sermon, and, after further devotions, were allowed to return to their homes, where more of the same awaited them. For what remained of the "day of rest," they were spied on by the master lest they should venture out of doors to stroll in the woods and lanes.[16] Are there in Galt's *Eben Erskine* disguised references to his short-lived Irvine schooldays – to capabilities in himself that his schoolfellows could not see? In the school Eben Erskine attended there were two schoolmasters, as at Irvine, but, Eben says, "with these professors I acquired no celebrity . . . my health was in those days infirm, and like all tall, growing boys, my intellects were rather, I suspect, deemed dull and of a wallow (drooping) and dowie (languid) nature." One of the two schoolmasters, a "fierce fiery little man, ever bouncing and stotting (jumping back and forth) with passion," took snuff and imbibed freely, yet was an effective teacher. Despite his vituperativeness and the "igneous flickering of his temper," he heard Eben patiently and pleased him by telling his mother that he understood better what he was taught than any of the other boys, though they made greater progress. [17]

Certain of the pupils attending the Grammar School in and around Galt's time made a name for themselves in the world, as all through life he so much desired to do: David Boyle who became Lord President of the Court of Session and Lord Justice General of Scotland, and who was a second cousin of Dr. William ("Tiger") Dunlop of whom more will be heard later; Henry Eckford, "the grand architect and designer of the American Navy"; two of the Hamiltons of Grange a few miles up the coast from Irvine, the most distinguished of whom was Alexander Hamilton who has already been referred to; and the future tenth and eleventh Earls of Eglinton whose estates were situated in the locality where John Galt's grandfather operated the waukmill, and whose kinsman, the Honourable Archibald Montgomerie recruited for service in Canada during the war of 1812 the regiment known as Montgomerie's Highlanders.

The interruption of the first, Irvine phase of Galt's formal education cut him off greatly from companionship with boys of his own age. Consequently, while others were at school, he was pretty much on his own, educating himself as best he could, closely observing everything that was going on around him and storing up impressions of those oddities of human nature that the reader of his novels of Scottish life and character finds so endlessly entertaining.

One of his diversions, "remarkable," as he says, "in one so young," was his frequent visits to some of the aged womenfolk who lived in the close behind his grandmother's house "to hear their tales and legends" – the "old widow, bent into a hoop" who lived alone and "spun out her low and wintry existence by her rock and tow" (spinning wheel). He often helped her with her work and "enjoyed strange pleasure in the narratives of her life and privations." Or the elderly relative he "was also very partial to," whose husband was blind. She had "some brimstone notions of religion, but much in her circumstances excited at once both compassion and laughter." Or the mother of Bryce Gilliland, who in her garrulous way would never tire of telling him of how, Bryce, all the family she had left, was carried off by the press gang and, when still young, won distinction and rose to a high place in the British Navy. On the wall alongside the sailors' loft in the parish church there was a tablet commemorating young Gilliland's "crowded hour of glorious life." He had been twelve years in the Navy when his conduct in several engagements came to the attention of Admiral (later Lord) Collingwood who had him promoted to the rank of first lieutenant. He was appointed afterwards Flag Lieutenant aboard the *Royal Sovereign,* and was first to fall in action at the Battle of Trafalgar.[18]

No less fascinating would be the story of Robert Boyd, another local boy, who having also been pressed into the Navy, transferred to the Army and by dint of hard work and perserverance reached the peak of his career as Sir Robert Boyd, K.C.B., Lieutenant-General and Governor of Gibraltar. He shared with General Elliott the honour of delivering Gibraltar from a combined French and Spanish attack in 1782.

In short, Galt in childhood was as he says of another of his own literary characters,

> distinguished from all the lads of his own age, for the preference which he gave to the knacky (meticulous) conversation of old and original characters. It signified not to him, whether the parties, with whom he enjoyed his leisure, were deemed douce (sedate) or daft (silly); it was enough that their talk was cast in queer phrases, and their minds ran among the odds and ends of things. By this peculiar humour, he was preserved in his clachan (village), simplicity; while he made . . . 'his memory like a wisdom-pock, a fouth (abundance) of auld (old) knick-knacketies – clues of experience, and shapings of matter, that might serve to clout (patch) the rents in the knees and elbows o'straits and difficulties.'[19]

He had a hobby of which he was particularly fond. Early one spring morning as he was playing in the garden at the back of the Galt house, he was surprised to see some narcissus shoots peeping above ground. He was taken shortly afterwards to Greenock to visit his mother's people and stayed there for a week or two. Darkness had fallen when he got back to Irvine, but rising at dawn next morning and going out into the garden he felt his curiosity excited at finding the narcissus in full bloom. From then on he was "passionately fond of flowers," and later manifested a "predilection for trees and shrubs." It may have been about then that he

21

received the gift of a laburnum tree which was sent to him by the lady who, as he tells us, was supposed to be the Eliza of Robert Burns.

When not otherwise occupied he would be in his regular outdoor haunts – the wooded banks of the secluded stream that flowed past the Howemill; or the Goffields (Golffields) on the steep side of Irvine Water to the south of the parish church; or the churchyard. There was a short cut from the Goffields to the town centre through the churchyard and people who came and went that way must have wondered at the boy so often seen among the tombstones. What could so interest him there? The churchyard interested him greatly, indeed, fascinated him, for it was for him a sort of outdoor history book containing further "clues of experience, and shapings of matter" which, with the other sights and sounds of his waking hours would pass before him at the day's end, as his thoughts hovered on the borderland of sleep, or come back to him in his dreaming while he slept.

The wide view westward from the moor at the north end of the town – another of his haunts – extends from high above the river, over the grassy flats to the harbour, the sand dunes and the sea and, in the distance, the wide sweep of the horizon. The scene is brought before us in Galt's vivid description of it at the close of a summer day:

> It was a beautiful evening: the sun set in all his glory beyond the hills of Arran; and the peak and summits of Goatfield,[20] covered with a fine aerial haze, glowed, as it were, with an internal principle of splendour. The sea in the bay of Ayr lay like molten gold, and Ailsa rose empurpled in the distance like a magnificent amethyst; while the whole coast, from the towers of Culzeen (sic) to the promontory of Ardrossan, glittered with towns and villages, and the seats of many, who . . . had returned home to enjoy the fruits of their prosperous adventures.[21]

It is evident that the glories of nature made a powerful impression on him, but he was just as much impressed by the dwellings of those who "had returned home to enjoy the fruits of their prosperous adventures." The splendour of the summer sun going down on the horizon! Ah, yes, but over the horizon what other splendours might there be, what further prospects of "prosperous adventures," what beckoning paths to dreams of youth that one day might come true? Galt, looking back years later probably to that very scene and the thoughts it awakened in him, wrote:

Peneus! as on thy green side
  A pensive hour I chanced to spend,
Where, o'er thy gaily flowing tide

22

The beeches bow and osiers bend;

. . . .

Me thought that youth was still my own
As when I strayed by Irvine's stream,
    And all the cares I since have known
The phantoms of a troubled dream,
    Ah! never shall I know again
Those simple hopes of blithesome hue,
    The playmates gay of fancy's train,
Such as by Irvine's stream I knew.[22]

The weakness Galt complained of in his childhood – an "all-overishness" as he called it – caused him to spend a good deal of his time lying on his bed, devouring the literary wares peddled from door to door by packmen – *Chevy Chase, Leper the Tailor,* and the like.[23] His mother, however, could not bear to see his sleepy nature and ascribed it to his being so much taken up with books. "In after life," he remarked, "when she was old and circumstances had changed, she confessed her error; but it cannot be accounted for in a woman so remarkably endowed.[24] Under her superintendence I undoubtedly made great moral proficiency; . . . but she was angrily averse to my bookish propensities, and until I left the shelter of the maternal wing never ceased to condemn my drowsy studies."[25] Her ambition for him is perhaps epitomized in the words addressed by Mr. Macindoe to Bogle Corbet, in Galt's novel of that name:

Glasgow's the place for you. So ye see, prepare yourself: ye'll wear a green apron, and mebbe in time, grow lank and lantern-jawed . . . By and by ye'll stand on the plain-stanes, cheek by jowl with King William,[26] and I hope in time to see you with as big a belly and as heavy a purse as the rest of them . . .

Everything points to the fact that Galt's mother was the dominant influence in his early, most impressionable years. He fully acknowledged this when he wrote:

From my very childhood it had been my greatest delight to please this affectionate parent, and in consequence her loss weakened, if I may say, the motive that had previously impelled my energies. The world to me was deprived of one that I was actuated by an endeavour to gratify, and in proportion the charm of life was diminished in its power . . .

Many years before I had lost my father; but although few could have stronger claims on the reverence of their children than those to which he was entitled, there is a difference in the filial love which belongs to the father, from that which the child's heart thinks is the mother's due. The one is allied to esteem, friendship, and respect, but the other is a gentle feeling composed of confidence, kindness, and gratitude.[27]

On December 12, 1825, he wrote to his sister as follows:

Of the state of our poor mother I need say nothing, and it will now be out of my power to see her again . . . I had hoped that as some little compensation for the long arrear of obligations I had incurred to my mother, that she would have been spared to see me placed in some steadfast, and reputable situation, but it has pleased God to order it otherwise . . . it is the character of my fate to be a succession of cloud and sunshine, and in the changes there has ever been something to prevent me even in the darkest moments from yielding to despondency.[28]

"Cloud and sunshine" – they were present throughout his, as through everybody's life, but the sunshine seemed brighter and the clouds less menacing when his thoughts dwelt on the days spent "by Irvine's silvery stream." Abiding memories of those days are gathered up and enshrined in one of his best poems, with part of which this chapter may be brought appropriately to a close.

How beautiful! – not childhood's glad blue eyes
Are half so beautiful as shine the skies,
Mirror'd in yonder calm and summer flow –
A radiant vista of a noon below:
As if the Universe – the Infinite –
Were one bright vast of sunshine and delight;
And the great globe, with all that it inherits,
Hung in a halo form'd of glorious spirits.

Why hymns sad Fancy thus on solemn wing?
And Mem'ry back to me would boyhood bring,
Ere care I knew, when I might freely rove
The green Goffields, or sylvan Howmills grove –
The skyey vision in the witches' linn?
I then had visions too – alas! as thin.

But wayward, pensive, more I lov'd to muse –
Tranc'd in the churchyard, and the tombs peruse: –
At one I sadden'd, half inclin'd to flee,
Which spectral said, "Prepare to follow me!"
For I had heard that none in life may know,
To where, with Death, the dead hereafter go,
And often wonder'd, in the grim of night,
To what dread land the dead-man did invite.

Well I remember all the golden prime,
When sleep and joy were night and day in time,
That to be drowsy on my mother's knee
Was almost sweeter than blest liberty –
Oh! how my heart enjoy'd the lov'd caress,
The patted cheek, the fond maternalness;
And that soft blessing, Heaven could not but hear,
While on my neck fell the delightful tear.

Oft in the trances of my wond'ring youth,
When life was light, and hope believ'd as truth,
On the green hill I lov'd to muse alone,
Where gold-ey'd daisies bright around me shone,
And think, in innocence of boyhood, then,
How all was lovely that was made for men.

Oh! never more must I again behold
Such sunny days as were so bright of old,
When she that's dust embrac'd her wayward own,
And all the claims upon me were unknown.

My native burgh, its window-eyes so bright,
Basks in the noon, and purrs as with delight –
Sweet is the thought, as in that hour of ease,
When all of life was but to play or please.
Mysterious Nature! why should he complain,
Who plays a child in memory's hall again,
Who sees around him, ever bright and fair,
The hopes of life, though but a picture's there;
And with the past, when griefs and cares annoy,
May be again a happy-hearted boy.[29]

Chapter 2

ROADS OF DESTINY

By the last decade of the eighteenth century Greenock was beginning to take a leading place in the new era of commercial development resulting from the increase of trade with the American colonies. Its rise to prominence in the age of steam was signalled by the fact that it was the birthplace of James Watt whose improved version of the Newcomen engine later was made use of by George Stephenson to drive the first railroad locomotive. There were obviously good economic reasons for Captain Galt's moving with his family to Greenock in 1789. He had acquired part-ownership in a West Indiaman with Greenock as its home port, and had decided to relinquish his role of master mariner for that of merchant ashore, as witness the following entry in the Greenock shipping registry for April 1791:

> These are to certify that James Pirrie is now become Master of the within named Ship Elizabeth in the Room of John Galt late Master of said Ship.

Galt could remember standing, when a boy, on the West Quay at Greenock holding his father by the finger while the latter was in conversation with a local banker and shipbuilder who laid down the keel of the ship that Captain Galt commanded until he left the sea. It was the beginning of a new and important chapter in Galt's life, although to begin with he was not particularly impressed by his new surroundings. As he remarked in the *Autobiography*:

> My removal to Greenock was neither heralded nor attended by comets or eclipses; I forget everything about it, except that the family took up their abode in a new house which my father had built . . . attached was a garden, in the decorations of which my taste for flowers suffered no interruption.[1]

There was a good deal of lee way to be made up where his formal education was concerned. He attended the school in the Royal Close where Colin Lamont taught writing and mathematics as well as training many of the Clyde shipmasters in navigation, geography and the like. Of his Greenock schooldays Galt said:

> At the schools if I was not considered a dull boy I certainly made no particular progress. That softness of disposition which arose from languor was perhaps not so remarkable there as at Irvine, for I recollect my experience of increased vigour. It never however acquired at Greenock the epithet of equanimity such as I afterwards enjoyed in the world, . . .[2]

It could not then be said of Greenock, as it was said of Irvine, that the educational facilities were particularly good. G. J. Weir in his *Recollections of Galt* declared that Galt and his generation were unfortunate in being schooled at Greenock as classical education was low about that period.[3] Nevertheless, as time went on, Galt became conscious of a budding of his faculties, no doubt due in large measure to the special attachment – "the Triumvirate" he called it – which grew up between him and two lads in the town, James Park and William Spence, the former a year and the latter two years older than himself. By his widely acclaimed treatise on Logarithmic Trancendants, Spence, when still quite a young man, gave evidence of a genius for mathematics. His promising career was, however, cut off in 1810 by his untimely death. Galt persuaded Sir John Herschel the distinguished scientist to contribute the preface for a posthumous volume of Spence's writings on mathematical subjects, and wrote for it a memoir of his friend in which he related some of their boyish efforts in experimental science. It was most likely from Spence that Galt acquired his "taste for mechanics" of which, in his early Greenock days, he has given the following examples:

> I was a sort of a fisher, but never distinguished. The scene of my reveries was a considerable stream in the moors behind the mountains above the town. It has since been brought round the shoulder of the hill, and being dammed up, it now by a canal gives to the town a valuable water power. Among my fishing dreams this very improvement, in a different manner, was one of the earliest.
>   In the Firth, opposite to Greenock, there is a large sand bank often dry at low water. When it was proposed to enlarge the harbour it occurred to me that this bank might be converted into land, and I have still a very cheap and feasible plan for gradually doing it, but unfortunately the bank belonged to the crown and was too sacred to

be improved. . . . long after I had left the town, the Barons of the Exchequer were induced to give the bank to the town for a mess of pottage in the shape of a cask of rum; the town has not however yet made use of the acquisition nor evinced any sense of its value: some day the magistrates under a reformed parliament will no doubt be enlightened on the subject.[4]

In this connection George Douglas Brown, an Ayrshire-born writer, said of Galt:

Imagination may consecrate the world to a man, or it may merely be a visualising faculty which sees that as already perfect which is still lying in the raw material. The Scot has the lower faculty in full degree; he has the forecasting leap of the mind which sees what to make of things – more, sees them made and in vivid operation. To him there is a railway through the desert where no railway exists, and mills along the quiet stream. And his *perfervidum ingenium* is quick to attempt the realizing of his dreams. That is why he makes the best of colonists. Galt is his type – Galt, dreaming in boyhood of the fine water power a fellow could bring round the hill, from the stream where he went a-fishing (they have done it since), dreaming in manhood of the cities yet to rise amid Ontario's woods (they are there to witness to his foresight).[5]

In 1795, when he was sixteen, Galt entered the Greenock Customs House to improve his penmanship and prepare himself for a mercantile career. At the end of the following year he was taken on by Messrs James Miller and Company, who were agents for several vessels engaged in the Canada trade, as a junior clerk at the quays. Eventually, through the influence of his father who had started up the firm of Gordon and Company of Glasgow, he entered into partnership with Ewing, Miller's nephew. It was, according to Alexander Rodger, the opinion of parties well able to judge of it, that Galt's prospects in embarking on a mercantile career were very favourable and that his attainment of the partnership with Ewing, under all the circumstances, betokened considerable talent and merit on his part.[6]

There was a specially close bond between Galt and James Park who for a time had worked, like Galt, in the local customs house. It was G. J. Weir's opinion that in any biography of Galt honourable mention should be made of Park who, in Weir's estimation, was "a person of excellent abilities, greatly improved by self-cultivation." Alexander Rodger, who affirmed that from the first Galt thought himself overlooked in Greenock, and who was personally inclined to think that to a certain extent he was, wrote:

> Park was the only man with whom Galt softened his tone in conversational debate. Park had paid homage to his genius; . . . It was almost surprising to see the towering disposition of the other bending before him; and at times calmly submitting to argumentative defeat. His influence over, and for the good of Galt, I consider to have been very great. . . . The two were ever together, and assisting each other in their . . . enterprises and evincements of public spirit, through which they made themselves first known among their compeers and townsmen . . . I have seen a graceful vine entwining itself around a noble forest tree; covering its rough bark and gnarled knots with beautiful leaves and clustering fruit, and ever swaying and bending its hardy boughs through its tendril entwinements, – to something of this kind I love to liken the friendship of Park and his friend Galt.[7]

Galt and Park studied languages together. Galt's reading, of which he was doing a great deal, had awakened in him a desire to learn Italian and, for want of a suitably qualified local teacher, he undertook to teach himself. R. P. Gillies, a writer contemporary with Galt said of him that he was educated exclusively for pursuits of trade and commerce, that he made no pretension to scholarly attainments, and that in literary capacity he was self-educated.[8] Indeed, one can hardly escape the impression that the leisure-time activities in which Galt engaged with Spence and Park as well as other Greenock youths of his own age – the musical evenings, the monthly Literary/Debating Society, the visits to the theatre in Glasgow, the outdoor excursions such as the boat trip to Loch Lomond and the annual walking tours – were to a large extent devised by Galt as exercises in self-improvement.

Amongst the "evincements of public spirit" previously mentioned was the Greenock Library affair which, as Galt reported it, occurred during the French Revolution when party spirit was running high. The library management committee getting caught up in the general excitement, resolved at a public meeting to have certain books considered tainted by revolutionary teaching withdrawn from circulation and placed for safe keeping in the custody of Mr. John Dunlop, the grandfather of Dr. William ("Tiger") Dunlop. To counteract this move which greatly angered the young men connected with the library, and Galt to an even greater extent, a plot was hatched in which he was the ringleader. He recalled that at the library annual general meeting whoever happened to be in the chair nominated the members of the library committee and his nomina-

30

tions were accepted. Things were, therefore, so arranged that the chairman at the next general meeting was a gentleman, later appointed a magistrate, who took good care that the liberals should be in the majority. The result was that not only were the banned books recalled, but the annual subscription rate was raised in order to purchase more and from then on the liberals in the town had the upper hand in the management of the library.[9]

There is also an incident connected with two volunteer companies, or the Corps of Gentlemen Sharpshooters as they were called, which besides being the first of their kind raised in Britain were raised by Galt himself ably supported by his friend Park. The services of the volunteers were not at first accepted by the War Office, so they held a meeting and adopted a resolution proposed by Galt to the effect that, having been persuaded of the danger to which the country was exposed by the threat of invasion by Napoleon, they had banded themselves together and made as generous an offer as any other volunteer group in the kingdom. However, they now rejoiced to hear that their fears had no foundation and would, therefore, on being assured by his Majesty's government that this was the case, retire into private life and exert themselves to counteract the false alarm which was being put about. The resolution was sent to the War Office and had an immediate effect; the corps and its officers were listed in the next military gazette.[10]

Up to this point there is no evidence to indicate that Galt was not enjoying life at Greenock or that he was not happy in his work. He acknowledged that the years he spent in James Miller and Company's office were "bright to look back upon." Yet, in spite of that, he suddenly severed his connection with the firm. It must have been quite a bombshell to his family and friends. Indeed, the events leading up to it hardly seemed to justify his taking such a step. One of the company's Glasgow clients addressed to them a somewhat abusive letter which was handed to Galt in the counting-house near to closing time. When he read it his "blood boiled." Determined to have it out with the "purse-proud" Glasgow man, he sent for Ewing, Miller's nephew, and announced what he had decided to do. The following morning he set off on a chase that took him first to Glasgow, then to Edinburgh where, at 9.00 in the evening, he ran down his quarry at the Turf Coffee House and forced him to hand over a written apology. It was almost midnight before Galt left Edinburgh intending to go right back to Greenock. During the return journey, however, many things crossed his mind and on a sudden impulse he changed course and made for Irvine. From there he informed Ewing and his parents of his intention to quit Greenock. His parents went to him immediately. They had a letter for him from Ewing, but nothing they or Ewing had to say could induce him to change his mind.[11]

Galt was never really in his element at Greenock. Although he had formed a strong attachment to the town, he felt constrained by his environment; but could that have been a sufficiently compelling reason for his throwing up his situation in which, according to Rodger, had he held on to it, he would most likely have grown rich and certainly become one of the influential or great men of the place? The encounter with the Glasgow client was, as Galt admitted, only the "proximate cause" of his decision to end the partnership with Ewing. Something of a more traumatic nature must have happened to make Galt, whatever he felt about the Greenock environment, break abruptly with the close, personal ties there that meant so much to him, and set off on what seemed a wild goose chase to London. The clue to all this may be found in the following statement which appeared some years after Galt's death in a Greenock newspaper:

> For half a century the late John Galt kept in his desk, never seen by human eye save his own, the miniature of a young lady . . . . The likeness was taken when the lady was about to proceed to the south of England for the benefit of her health: but the hope of lengthened day from the change of climate was doomed to be disappointed, as she there died. During his varied career, our clever townsman seems ever to have retained fresh in his memory a tender recollection of her who first called forth his affection. Very shortly before his death, Mr. Galt gave the portrait to his friends, with directions that it might be presented to some one of the relatives of the lady who had not any other remembrance of her, and this wish was complied with.[12]

The young lady in question was the sister of John Henderson,[13] one of the group accompanying Galt on the boat trip to Loch Lomond. Perhaps it was with reference to her that Galt wrote:

> When the golden light is fading
> From yon far seen mountain's crest,
> All our joyous valley shading,
> Love and sadness fill my breast.
> Star of Love! that saw us parted,
> Shall we never meet again?
> Shall I ever broken-hearted,
> Fondly sigh, and sigh in vain?[14]

Although Galt had made up his mind definitely to go to London, he did not act on his decision until many months had passed. Nothing is known of what happened to him or what he was doing in the interval. Eventually on a May morning in 1804, accompanied by his father, he boarded the post-chaise which was to take him to Glasgow early enough to meet the London coach, and he bade farewell to Greenock. The air was calm and bright but he felt terribly depressed. While the horses were being changed halfway between Greenock and Glasgow, he walked across the fields to the brow of a nearby hill, and, as he looked toward Argyleshire it seemed to him as if some pensive influence resting on the mountains was alluring him silently back. He returned to the halting place and the journey was resumed. His obstinacy, he reflected, had been "too indulgently considered"; he was not blind to the perils awaiting him;[15] he felt that in his London adventure he had thrown himself like a die from the dice-box.[16] He and his father put up at the Globe Tavern in Fleet Street in London, where Galt planned to stay as long as his father remained in town. His father in due course took leave of him. Now he was on his own, with "neither friend nor acquaintance, a forlorn adventurer as well could be." His reflections may have resembled those of Mr. Ezekiel, the "bonnet laird" in *Eben Erskine,* who tells the story of *The Schoolmaster's Register,* with its account of the boys who at various times had passed through the schoolmaster's hands, and of their careers, both at school and afterwards: the lad of ordinary ability in whose advancement fate always seemed to play a part, who rose from humble beginnings to become governor of an island, a member of Parliament, the richest of the rich; and the brighter, wiser, more kindly affectioned, but more careless type among his contemporaries who lived a life of unrewarding labour and who died leaving his wife and children in poverty. Galt, like Eben Erskine, may have found comfort in the thought that the circumstances in which he might be placed would call forth any talent that he had and that, as he acted in those circumstances, he might make himself great or famous.

He spent the first six months in London in a desultory sort of way – reading, sightseeing, going to the theatre and filling his mind with such knowledge as might prove useful in the mercantile profession. With that in view, he mastered the Lex Mercatoria and produced a treatise on the practice of underwriting (marine insurance), but destroyed the manuscript when he thought of how hopeless his prospects in life appeared to be. He wrote a history of the ancient commerce of England down to and inclusive of the reign of George the Third, and one on bills of exchange; studied political economy and followed up the free trade question but, despite his being "indefatigably industrious," he never ceased to regret his misspent time, for it was "but barren toil."

Park corresponded with him regularly and Galt often stood much in need of his advice. Park more than anyone influenced his decision to withdraw from circulation his recently published Gothic poem, "The Battle of Largs" which he had brought with him to London in the expectation that it would open for him the door to fame and fortune. It was all very well, as Mr. Adage in Galt's *Bogle Corbet* says, for doctors, clergymen and lawyers to write books, but for a man bred to commerce of any kind to attempt more is high treason in the republic of letters. Galt, nevertheless, was coming round gradually to think of literature as "only a means" but, for all that, a means "of influence," which in his case eventually it certainly proved to be.

He struck up an acquaintance with a Mr. James Hamilton "who, in addition to superior qualifications for business, united a remarkable taste for family history and heraldry with a bias for the finer workings of the mind." From him Galt acquired a knowledge of families, their descents, and their connections, which made him "seem learned in that hieroglyphical (sic) language to many who affect to have studied it more." Ever the typical utilitarian Scot, he was doubtless able to use to good effect the "rare, recondite things of heraldry" he picked up from Hamilton, when, later on, he was making his way in the *beau monde* of London society.

Galt also discovered a certain aptitude in himself for acting the role of professional lobbyist. What one might call his first case in that capacity concerned a Mr. Archibald Thomson, engineer and inventor of an apparatus for making ropes. A flaw had been found in an agreement into which Thomson had entered. He went to Lord Erskine, with whom he was acquainted, for advice, and was told that he should first of all get someone to prepare a statement of what was involved. Thomson applied to Galt who had previously been of service to him and Galt drew up the statement. Everything worked out to Thomson's satisfaction, and to repay Galt he offered him one of the shares in his latest project – constructing the first steamboat for the Thames. Galt, however, declined the offer as he considered it out of all proportion to the service he had rendered.[17]

When he left Greenock Galt carried in his trunk "a whole mail of introductory letters" to various people in London. It soon became evident when he went round delivering them that the most he could expect from them was "an occasional free dinner." There was no other course but to put his own best foot forward, so he began to look about him. Before long he found what he thought was the right connection in the person of "a delicate young man" called McLachlan from his own part of the country,

34

whom he considered eminently suitable as a business associate. In 1805, they went into business together as factors, brokers, dealers and chapmen. Galt's father contributed the capital required to launch this venture. It appears that included with the capital went an agency for the house of Messrs Still, May and Company of Greenock, worth, according to Weir, £800 annually in commissions.

Galt in his novel *Bogle Corbet* spoke of "a pre-ordered arrangement" that "inscrutably exists between the fortunes of individuals" and of "accidental meetings with particular persons" that "are always followed by good or ill fortune." His meeting with McLachlan was certainly for the worst, for when their "most sanguine expectations" of success seemed about to be fulfilled, McLachlan was found to be insolvent and Galt had to bail him out. Things continued fairly uneventfully from then on until, after they had been three years in business, Galt and McLachlan found themselves in difficulties because of the financial embarrassment of one of their correspondents. Knowing that his own hopes for the future and his father's comfort in old age were at stake, Galt exerted himself to the utmost to save the situation. He travelled to Greenock and elsewhere to see what could be done to patch things up when word came that a firm with which he and McLachlan were involved was on the verge of collapse. Still, May and Company foreclosed toward the end of 1807. Galt and McLachlan therefore, had no alternative but to file for bankruptcy.

This was embarrassing enough for Galt financially and in other respects as well. His way of looking on Greenock, in Rodger's opinion, and on what most of his associates there valued so highly, excited something like hostility to his advancement and his fame, which gave rise in turn to asperities on his part. Matters were not mended when Galt's financial difficulties brought him once more into contact with his old Greenock acquaintances. Many of them felt that at one time they had been under-rated by him, but having chosen and persevered in plainer paths, they in their turn now began to plume themselves in comparing their position in life with his.[18]

Despite the harassment and humiliation of having to file for bankruptcy, Galt at the beginning of 1809 tried his hand again at business, with his brother Tom as partner. He may have done so under pressure from the family who, presumably, had maintained him during his first six months in London, and for whom Tom's future was now a matter of some concern. By an unexpected turn of events, however, soon after the new partnership was formed, Tom decided to seek his fortune in Honduras. On May 18, 1809, while the preparations for Tom's departure were in progress, Galt "entered" himself "of Lincoln's Inn," that is to say, took steps to qualify as a lawyer. This sudden move took everyone by surprise. His next move was almost as sudden, and even more surprising. Partly for health reasons and partly to put in his time before being called to the bar, he went off to the continent.

He had all his life perhaps a tendency to over dramatize a situation. The European tour, as he described it, marked an unpleasant, indeed, a bitter crisis in his life; he "was about to be born," as he put it, "into the scene of a new world in which there was no reason to expect that his chequered destiny would be changed." He realized how young he was, and how ignorant of the world, yet felt himself fit for anything he was likely to undertake, and not liable to be daunted easily.[19] He was, therefore, neither particularly elated nor particularly depressed when the packet on which he was a passenger cleared Falmouth harbour, with its course set for Gibraltar.

His *Voyages and Travels* (1812) and *Letters from the Levant* (1813) contain a great mass of commercial handbook and travel diary material. In what follows as regards his wanderings and adventures on the continent the spotlight is allowed to fall only on some of the more colourful or dramatic incidents, as narrated in the *Autobiography*.[20]

On the day of his arrival at Gibraltar, Galt went to the garrison library. While he was reading there a young man entered and sat down at a table opposite him. His face, which seemed familiar to Galt, was prepossessing and intelligent, conveying an impression of elegance and character. Galt was one of a numerous party invited to dine that evening with the secretary of the fortress. Tom Sheridan who, with his wife and the Countess of Westmorland was also present, mentioned that Lord Byron and Mr. Hobhouse, the translator of classical poetry, had come in from Spain intending to proceed up the Mediterranean. Later on, at Gibraltar, while embarking for Sardinia, Galt saw among the passengers the person who had attracted his attention in the garrison library. It was none other than Lord Byron.

When the ship put in at Cagliari, a dinner reception was given by the British Minister, followed by a night at the theatre. After the performance, the Minister came down with Byron to the gate of the upper town where, at leave-taking, Byron thanked him loquaciously (in your "harlotry players" style, as Galt put it) to the amusement of Hobhouse and the others looking on. Byron was afterwards made the target for a good deal of banter from his friends, but, fancying that he had acquitted himself well, grew petulant. Hobhouse walked on ahead, and Byron whose lameness and the rough pavement were giving him difficulty, took Galt by the arm and asked him appealingly if he could have said less than he did to the Minister for the kindness they had received. Galt assured him that he could not and from then on "was more distinguished by" Byron's "familiarity," though Byron "claimed more deference" than Galt was disposed to grant.

His travels brought him to Athens. Byron and Hobhouse happened to be there, and Hobhouse called on Galt and induced him to renew his acquaintance with Byron. It was about this time that the commotion arose over Lord Elgin's removal from the Greek temples of the marbles that came to be named after him. Galt wrote a longish poem in mock heroic style on this outrage to Minerva, but he was also in the ploy, was, indeed, within an ace of acquiring the marbles himself when, just in the nick of time, Lord Elgin's agent intervened.

While reading an Italian newspaper at Tripolitza, where he spent two days before getting into Athens, Galt hit on the idea of setting up an establishment somewhere in the Levant to counteract the effect of the Berlin and Milan Decrees promulgated by Napoleon for imposing a blockade on the export of British manufactures to the continent. What Galt particularly had in mind was a location which would serve as a base for running the blockade or in effect smuggling the forbidden manufactures into Europe. He was convinced that the scheme would work and was soon busily engaged in getting it organized. Hydra or Zea (Kea) seemed likely places for a base or depot from which to operate. After inspecting them, however, Galt ruled out both for the same reason – they could not ensure the secrecy needed for the successful operation of his plan. A stranger with whom he got into conversation in a coffee house at Scios suggested that the island of Myconi might be better suited to his purpose. Galt lost no time in following up this suggestion. He chartered an open boat to take him to the island where he found something like what he was looking for – a mansion that Count Orloff had built as part of Catherine the Second of Russia's designs on the Archipelago and that at one time had been the residence of the Russian consul-general. Galt's scheme was beginning to mature when he was notified by Struthers, Kennedy and Company of Malta who were acting as his agents that a project similar to his own was, at the suggestion of one of their partners in Vienna, contemplated by Kirkman Finlay and Company of Glasgow. Since it was going to take time for Galt's agents to contact the Glasgow company to apprise them of his plan and get an answer back from them, he decided to continue his inspection of the coast around the Archipelago in order to ascertain the safest route to the borders of Hungary. On this expedition he was accompanied by a sightseeing gentleman bound for Constantinople.

The first stopping-place of any importance on their itinerary was Mar-
athonesi where they put up overnight in a house loaned them by a Greek.
They took ship next morning for Bathi and on landing there were met by
a scout and conducted to the castle of Anton Bey for whom Galt had letters of commendation.[21] The travellers were made welcome, hospitably
entertained, and invited to take part in a forthcoming boar hunt, which
they respectfully declined. They were given letters by Anton Bey recommending them to some of his friends who were Turkish governors. Bidding Bey farewell they proceeded to Mavroyuni and, with an overnight
halt at Tripolitza, made their way back to Athens. Having remained there
several days they resumed their journey via Marathon, Negropont,
Thebes, Livadia and Chaeronea to Parnassus. By the pass of Thermopy-
lae they gained Zeitun, then Phersela and Larissa, and rode down the
Vale of Tempe. Reaching the Gulf of Salonika they crossed over to Thessalonica. It seems that Galt was still on the lookout for the right spot on
which to set up his base of operations, for he noted that Thessalonica was
well suited to his purpose. Riding day after day "with almost insufferable
constancy" he and his companion reached Constantinople. There they
parted company and Galt was joined by Struthers of the Malta-based
firm of Struthers, Kennedy and Company, who was keen on cooperating
with him in his plan for counteracting the Berlin and Milan Decrees.
They crossed the north limb of Asia Minor and got as far as Kirpi.

By this time, however, Galt had come to the conclusion, and Struthers
was inclined to agree, that the excursion was not contributing a great deal
to the furtherance of the plan. They, therefore, decided to return to Constantinople. Galt then arranged for a hundred bales of merchandise to be
sent on camels to Vidin, while he went on ahead to make preparations for
depositing them there till such time as it might be possible to get them
shipped via Orsova to Hungary. The journey to Vidin in wintertime
through largely unmapped territory, and with the Russians swarming all
over the countryside, was anything but inviting. Hardships and hazards,
however, seemed to have no power to daunt Galt, for he had in those
days, as he tells us, "a physical enjoyment in enterprise."

Leaving Constantinople on this hazardous undertaking in the middle
of the first week of January, 1810, Galt travelled to Adrianople where he
was treated to galas and dances by the French residents. He went on from
there to Philippi, seldom halting beyond that point till he found himself
in Sofia the headquarters of Vilhi Pasha whom he called on soon after his
arrival, to seek protection for himself and the caravan with the bales of
merchandise for Vidin coming up behind. Vilhi Pasha proved most coop-
erative. He provided Galt with a military escort and with an envoy bear-

ing credentials which would ensure Galt safe passage along the route to his destination.

It was late in the evening when Galt reached Vidin, and, although it was against military regulations to do so, the archbishop to whom he had letters "of particular recommendation," put him up. Mula Pasha the local potentate had been informed of Galt's arrival and speedily summoned the archbishop to account for his visitor. Meanwhile the Pasha's interpreter who had remained behind with Galt in his room at the archbishop's residence, got suspicious and set Galt down as a spy. This surprised Galt very much, as the red waistcoat he was wearing was the only thing he could think of as giving rise to such an astonishing idea. It was not so very surprising really. When Galt was on the point of setting out for Vidin the talk in certain quarters was that he had been sent from England on some private political mission, in short, that he was a secret agent working for the British government.

Early in the morning after his arrival Galt was also summoned to appear before Mula Pasha, his promotion having in the meantime (he recorded facetiously) been more rapid than is usual in the military, for he was now regarded and addressed as a general. The visit, as it turned out, passed off civilly enough. Galt was, however, advised after the visit not to stay more than three days in the town and to refrain from walking round the fortifications.[22]

The envoy detailed at Sophia to accompany Galt to Vidin was then hailed before Mula Pasha, and on rejoining Galt implored him tearfully to tell him whether he was indeed a Russian spy, for, if so, Mula Pasha had threatened to have his head. He also told Galt that he had been ordered by Mula Pasha to submit to interrogation. Galt refused to let him be interrogated. This led to Galt himself being questioned and his papers investigated. Brazening it out, he calculated, might save the situation. He put on a bold front. The bluff worked, and the entire incident was apparently considered closed, for nothing more was heard of it.

A gentleman from Vienna (probably a partner or representative of Kirkman Finlay and Company) was supposed to be at Vidin to receive the consignment of merchandise when it arrived, but he failed to put in an appearance, having, as was learned later, decided not to go through with the transaction. This left Galt in a really serious predicament. With funds running out, he was beginning to get desperate. Just then, however, an escape route appeared out of the blue. Among Galt's guests one evening was an old Turk who happened to mention that in his boyhood he had been taken into the household of a Hungarian nobleman where for years he had been treated as a member of the family, and that he had vowed, as far as possible, on his return to Turkey, to repay the kindness he had received. He now came to Galt's assistance, told him that forty thousand piastres would be put at his command, paid off his expenses, and undertook to receive on delivery the consignment of merchandise.

The following day Galt left Vidin homeward bound. From Cagliari he proceeded to Gibraltar, then to Ireland, then to Scotland where he spent a few days in Greenock, and arrived back in London in the autumn of 1811 having seen much but, he confessed, accomplished little as men measure accomplishment. His Levant scheme had brought him no profit. Still, he considered himself fortunate to have got out as he did. He was now thirty-two years of age. Somewhere in the future lay the goal in life which he had yet to find. What was that goal to be?

Chapter 3

LIFE AMONG
THE "LIONS"

Back again in London, Galt felt that the time had come to take stock of his situation and give serious thought to the business of making a living. What of the legal profession? That would have to be ruled out. During the stopover at Greenock on his way back from the continent, he had learned that his brother's prospects in Honduras were far from promising. Consequently there was little likelihood of his brother being able to afford him the financial assistance he would need in order to prosecute his studies for the bar. Or the Levant scheme? Might something to his advantage not yet come of that? Just then he heard of the possibility of his receiving an appointment in connection with a proposal similar to the Levant scheme, which Sir Stratford Canning of the Foreign Office intended to submit to the government. Negotiations for the proposal, however, dragged on to the point at which that, too, looked like being a dead end, whereupon "indignant to observe how little attention was paid . . . to an object evidently important," Galt called at the Foreign Office and left the person he spoke to there in no doubt as to how he felt about such bureaucratic indifference.[1] This was the first but by no means the last occasion on which he showed how anything but "bird-mouthed" he could be in his dealings with governmental officialdom.

It would be about this time that he became more acquainted with a London-Scot called Alexander Tilloch, with whose fortunes his own were to be closely intertwined in the not far distant future. "I approve of your confidence in Tilloch," Park had written to him from Greenock on October 30, 1805. "The friendship of such a man is worth cultivating; and certainly a real friendship always implies more than a mere community of speculative opinions. A confidential intimacy enables the partners to share each other's hopes and fears, which is undoubtedly the basis of all strong attachments."[2]

Tilloch was born on February 28, 1759 in Glasgow and was a graduate of its ancient university. In 1782 he and Andrew Foulis, Jr., the printer to the university patented a perfected version of Ged's achievements in stereotyping (the art of producing books from plates instead of from moveable type). In 1787 Tilloch migrated to London where he purchased *The Star,* an evening newspaper, which he edited for the next thirty-four years. He established *The Philosophical Magazine* in 1797 and later incorporated it with *Nicholson's Journal of Natural History, Chemistry, and the Arts,* founded the same year as the magazine in which Galt made his *début* as an article writer with his "Essay on Commercial Policy" in 1805, followed in 1807 by his "Statistical Account of Upper Canada." Shortly before his death in 1825 Tilloch began editing *The Mechanic's Oracle.* He was an LL.D. of Marischal College, Aberdeen; an affiliate of the London Philosophical Society; and a member of the Royal Irish Academy. A picture of him shows a baldish, elderly and (an impression perhaps conveyed by the small-lensed spectacles he was wearing) an owlish-looking sort of man, but amiable and unpretentious as one would judge from his expression. He had long been a widower and, with an only daughter, Elizabeth, was living at Islington when Galt first got to know him. He loaned Galt books and manuscripts and it was through his influence that Galt gained access to the library of Jesus College, Oxford to do research for his *Life and Administration of Cardinal Wolsey.*

One has only to glance at the list of editors from Tilloch onward – Lawrence Bragg, Sir David Brewster, Michael Faraday, Sir William Herschel, Lord Kelvin, Sir Oliver Lodge, and G. P. Thomson among them – to appreciate the prestigious character of the *Philosophical.* It described itself on the title page of the first volume as "comprehending the various branches of science, the liberal and fine arts, agriculture, manufactures and commerce," its grand object being, as announced in the Preface, to diffuse philosophical knowledge among every class of society, and to give the public as early an account as possible of everything new and curious in the scientific world, both at home and on the continent.

Independently of his editorship of the magazine Tilloch had a broad range of interests. He wrote two books on Biblical subjects, and preached occasionally for the sect known as the Sandemanians. Without any practical engineering experience, he patented an "apparatus to be employed as a moving power to drive machinery" and "improvements to the steam engine or apparatus connected therewith." One of his most original achievements was his plan for the prevention of forgery in the form of a note which he engraved and submitted to the Bank of England in 1797, and which eminent engravers certified could not be copied. Little interest was shown in the idea at the time, but thirteen years later practically the same process was adopted for producing bank notes of the kind with which we are familiar nowadays.

Tilloch had three sisters living in Glasgow. The eldest, after whom his daughter was named, married the Reverend Dr. Burns, minister of the city church known as The Barony. Their son G. D. I. Burns later became prominently connected with the Cunard Steamship Line. Tilloch's younger sister was married twice, and when her second husband died, she and the youngest sister, who remained single, lived together. The latter is the "Aunt Tilloch" with whom Tilloch's daughter regularly corresponded throughout her adult life. Tilloch was probably one of those to whom Galt delivered the "whole mail of introductory letters" which he took with him to London, and one of the few among them who regarded the letter addressed to him as good for something more than a dinner ticket. He made Galt welcome in his home at 10 Barnsbury Street, Islington, which was then a "meeting place for many of the acutest minds of the day," perhaps for old time's sake, for it is just possible that the Tillochs and the Galts were closely acquainted. Captain Galt had been involved in the tobacco trade with Virginia in his seafaring days, and Tilloch's father was a fairly prosperous Glasgow tobacco merchant, judging by the "ample patrimony" he is said to have left his son.

Having as yet had no success in his search for permanent employment, Galt occupied himself with writing his *Voyages and Travels* which he decided to publish at his own risk. When the proof sheets were due to come off the press, Tilloch not only helped with the proofreading, but, while it was in progress, put Galt up at his house. How strange that Galt, so addicted as he was to what he called "metaphysical researches" or, in present-day phraseology, psychological analysis, could live under the same roof with Tilloch and his daughter yet have so little to say about the one, and nothing at all about the other. When the proofreading was completed Galt moved back into his lodgings, resolved on account of "the aspect of things" not being "very promising," to pursue "a very sequestered course of life." Lord Byron had returned from the continent and was living in the fashionable district around Picadilly Circus. On his way to the House of Lords he dropped in occasionally on Galt,[3] whom he had now come to think of as "a good philosophical fellow."

The *Voyages and Travels,* when it came off the press in 1812, got rough treatment from some of the critics. Galt was held up to ridicule in the May 1812 issue of the *Critical Review* as a Scotsman and a Presbyterian, and for not having received even "the mouthful of a grammar school education," obtainable in Scotland. Subsequently in the *Quarterly Review,* the *Monthly Review,* and the *British Critic,* the reviewers seized on something the rumblings of which would still be heard when Galt was in Upper Canada – his "censures on priestcraft," "hatred of Priesthood," his use of the expression "ecclesiastical locusts," his "malicious sneers levelled against the clergy," and his animadversions "against official ignorance" in treaty negotiations, which, it was said, had given offence. He was made out to be a Whig, and was alleged to be a member of a large and flourishing sect that considered its famous minister heaven-born.[4]

It took only the first of these criticisms to make Galt give up "all expectation of receiving any hitch of help in literature, more than in business." He learned about this time that there was a most profitable, secret commercial intercourse going on in the route he had opened up to Vidin. The news pleased but also pained him because many things about the project convinced him that he might have good thoughts, but had not the luck to carry them into effect. His blockade running enterprise on the continent was no merely hare-brained idea on his part. If it had been, Sir Stratford Canning would not subsequently have proposed something similar to the government. In his continental project Galt, working practically single-handed, was one jump ahead of Kirkman Finlay and Company of Glasgow. For his services in that connection, Kirkman Finlay, the head of the Glasgow firm, was well regarded by the government.

While Galt was still in a "state of fluctuating feeling" over the recent news from Vidin, Finlay approached him to find out if he would be interested in a scheme which his company had devised for counteracting the influence of the Berlin and Milan Decrees. He invited Galt to take charge of an agency which the company, as part of the scheme, was setting up at Gibraltar then being over-run by the French. Galt accepted but, before crossing over to the continent, took a notion – one wonders why – to go to Scotland to revisit all his old Irvine and Greenock haunts.

He had not been long at Gibraltar when he came to the conclusion that in the agency he had taken on he would be out of his element. Never in his life, he confessed, had he been able to lay his heart to anything in which the imagination did not play a part. The agency question, however, was settled for him by events beyond his control. The Duke of Wellington's victorious career in the Peninsula and his entry into Madrid on August 12, 1812 ended the Kirkman Finlay scheme. Since there was no "decent pretext" for leaving immediately, Galt stayed on at Gibraltar. Finding some time later that he needed surgical treatment, he went back to London at the beginning of 1813. While on the continent he observed "the great armies then afoot," and reflected on what the effect on society would be when "such vast masses were broken up."[5] After the war, the streets of London teemed with disbanded soldiers and sailors. That set him wondering. Might there not be a refuge somewhere for those men who, "in spite of being pressed, and forcibly taken from all that was dear to them, bullied by their officers, . . . flogged nearly to death for comparative trifles, yet fought like lions, and laid the foundations of England's . . . prosperity"?[6] The memory of these things was still with him when his thoughts turned one day in the future to that "philanthropic dream" that took him, intent on realizing it, to Upper Canada.

After his return to London Galt had a visit from Prince Koslovsky whom he had met at Cagliari in the course of his travels on the continent. The Prince's indefatigable pursuit of knowledge kept Galt constantly engaged. Galt introduced him to Lord Byron and the three of them went to the Royal Institution to hear a lecture on poetry. During this period, Galt got married, an event alluded to in the *Autobiography* in the most casual manner imaginable: "While his highness (Koslovsky) was engaged on a tour in the country, I was married . . . on a Tuesday!" When exactly, and to whom? Galt simply leaves his readers guessing. The actual date of the marriage was April 23, 1813 and the bride was Alexander Tilloch's daughter, Elizabeth, then thirty-two years of age.

Writing to his sister "Nancy" from London on June 11, 1806, Galt had let her know what he considered estimable in a woman as a prospective wife. Romantic love? Definitely not! That is the "brainless affection." What is most to be extolled is the esteem in which a woman holds her husband. If Galt was still of the same mind when he married, it was just as well that his bride was at an age to have put behind her any thoughts of "love's young dream." He for his part was in his chronic state of impecuniosity. Early in the year prior to his marriage he had taken on the editorship of the *Political Review,* but after two months gave it up. In spite of the asperities of the critics, his *Voyages and Travels* had sold well, at least well enough to enable him to pay off the actual travel costs, out of his share of the profits. In 1812 appeared his *Life and Administration of Cardinal Wolsey* and his *Letters from the Levant.* He lost £100 on the one, and made £400 on the other. There was, however, according to Weir, a generous marriage settlement whereby Dr. Tilloch provided his son-in-law with an annual allowance and a fine, well furnished house. Galt himself later installed something like a footman in the shape of a man to open and shut the door. The house was in Tavistock Square, and, Pigott has it, "wit, beauty and fashion, talented public and literary characters, the élite of the Societies, and members of the nobility" congregated for the banquets given by the Galts while they were living there.[7] Among those on the visiting list were Prince Koslovsky; J. G. Lockhart, the well known

Scottish author who was then editor of the *Quarterly Review,* and member of the famous Blackwood Group to which Galt also latterly belonged; Dr. Samuel Parr, the noted classical scholar; and the Right Honourable Edward Ellice – Bear Ellice as he was called from his connection with the fur trade in Canada – Member of Parliament for Coventry and subsequently Secretary at the War Office.

The wife of a distinguished man, it has been said, can never be uninteresting, but of all the characters who are made to pass before us in the unfolding drama of Galt's career none is so difficult to visualize as the woman he married. This is due as much as anything to the fact that he had so little to say about her. What did she look like? What sort of person was she? How did she rate as wife and mother? "The tradition in the family," to quote Aberdein, "is that she was tall and fair."[8] According to Harriet Pigott who held literary conferences with Galt, Elizabeth Galt "had no possible pretensions to beauty." A head and shoulders study in colour of Elizabeth[9] shows reddish hair and dark blue eyes. The impression of shyness, submissiveness perhaps, given by the sideward tilt of the head and the somewhat dreamy look on the almost perfectly oval face is offset by the rather long, straight nose with the prominent nostrils, and the firm lines about the mouth. Miss Pigott, then, may not have been speaking the whole truth.

A Mr. John Campbell, one of the sundry people who provided material for the Galt biography that Miss Pigott planned to write but never wrote, affirmed in a gossipy letter to her from Greenock, bearing the date June 24, but not the year, that Galt's wife was injudicious and improvident. "Although I accuse her," Campbell wrote, "I think it would be a pity to publish such anecdotes during her lifetime; it would only hurt the feelings of her family and friends and draw on yourself the malice of a *clever,* ill-natured woman." Then he added: "I know her sway with her sons, especially the youngest, is absolute; she could make them believe anything."[10]

This is, in one respect at least, unfair to Elizabeth. Galt was extremely fond and, undoubtedly, much concerned about the welfare of his sons whose births occurred in close, perhaps, in view of his financial situation, uncomfortably close succession – John's on August 13, 1814, Thomas' on August 12, 1815, and Alexander's on September 6, 1817. It cannot, however, be said that Galt had much responsibility for his children's nurture and upbringing, considering his frequent absences from the domestic scene. There was, therefore, more reason to applaud than to censure Elizabeth, as Campbell seemed concerned to do, for her "sway" over her sons or, to put it in plainer language, for keeping a tight grip on the reins, when as often as not there was no one else to do it; and neither her sons nor the world, as events would show, were any the worse for what she taught them to believe.

As for what Miss Pigott called Elizabeth's "spineless and disgusting attitude" to her husband's "perseverance in the walks of literature" and her "opposition to his undertaking literacy chores" (a good many of which were imposed on him by Miss Pigott herself), Galt spoke appreciatively of his wife's advice and other indications of her interest in his literary work. Miss Pigott had to concede that Elizabeth had "excellent good sense and good judgment," while Mrs. Katherine Thomson in her *Recollections of Literary Characters* described her as humble, religious and self-distrustful, spoke of her unmeasured sympathy, her solicitude and her faithfulness as a partner, and speculated on how important she was to her husband and her sons.

Galt had not long been married when hs received word of the death of his brother Thomas at Honduras, an event which, he said, left "a cold vacancy in his bosom" and made him resolve to be no longer an adventurer. Nevertheless on May 2, 1814, he went off on a rather pointless trip to Paris, with a stop at Rouen en route "to see the state of the cotton manufactories in the suburb of Deville"; and for good measure took in Brussels, Antwerp and Amsterdam where he hobnobbed with Russian royalty at the theatre.[11]

In the years immediately following his marriage, Galt got involved in a number of schemes. The first of these schemes was aimed at replacing the somewhat tinselled productions at Covent Garden and Drury Lane with something more classical, and giving the efforts of budding playwrights who had suffered the humiliation of the rejection slip the recognition which he felt to be their due. These flowers of genius, born and left to blush unseen, with some of Galt's own dramatic works thrown in, were published by Colburn as *The New British Theatre.* The rubbishy material submitted to Galt, however, soon made him realize how right the unappreciative theatre managers had been, and the venture fizzled out.

Almost without pause he involved himself in raising funds, "afterwards employed in building and endowing the National Caledonian Asylum" for the education and support of children of soldiers and sailors of Scottish extraction who were ineligible for admission to the Greenwich and Royal Chelsea institutions. He had a salary of £300 per annum, and things appeared to be going well. The grand inaugural dinner brought in a lot of money and almost four hundred annual subscriptions. It was acclaimed as the most splendid function of the kind ever given in London, but it landed Galt in a lawsuit with the organizing committee over the bill for the musical part of the program and left him the poorer by

£270. After that came a project with a Glasgow firm committed to act as his London guarantor to ship goods to Jamaica, destined for the Spanish colonies. The colonies revolted, however, before the plan could take effect.

Such business problems forced Galt to give up the style of Tavistock Square. He moved with his family to Finnart, in the Greenock neighbourhood, where in his teens he had spent many happy days at the summer house owned by James Park's people. While Galt and his family were living there – "the most unsatisfactory" interlude in his whole life – the Union Canal Company asked him to sponsor a bill on their behalf for extra capital to complete a canal between Edinburgh and Glasgow, that had been established by Act of Parliament in 1817. He accepted the offer to work as lobbyist and, once back in London, he felt no inclination to return to Finnart.

Much of what he had undertaken so far had, indeed, proved "barren toil." He toiled on, nevertheless, at the "secondary pursuit" of literature turning out a lot of hack work mostly, under a variety of pseudonyms. Between 1820 and 1823, however, he was producing some of the best things he ever did – *The Ayrshire Legatees* and *The Entail*. The manuscript of his masterpiece, *Annals of the Parish* which Constable had rejected in 1813 was accepted by William Blackwood, the Edinburgh publisher. He was beginning to be acclaimed as a writer worthy of attention. It looked as if he had arrived. The best proof was his admission to the famous circle which grew up in London around the Earl and Countess of Blessington.[12] Galt's interest in the theatre may have first brought him to the notice of the Earl of Blessington who had a flair for theatricals, and who, as Byron said, "with a numerous acquaintance, and 'all appliances to boot', for choosing and selecting, has found so much to like in Galt, *malgré* the difference of their politics, that his liking has grown into friendship."[13] According to Miss Pigott, the Earl, like Ellice and Lockhart, rendered Galt "essential services" out of pure esteem for his probity and talents. The character of Lord Sandiford in Galt's *Sir Andrew Wylie* is modelled on Blessington to whom the second edition of the work was dedicated. Little wonder that Galt regarded "that excellent bodie, Sir Andrew W." as "not the least" of his influential friends, even though as he said on one occasion when writing to Blackwood, Andrew was of a species somewhat similar to the Whigs and he ran hazard enough in its being supposed that Andrew represented himself. "Sir Andrew" was in fact the means whereby Galt came to be favoured with the friendship of royalty. On a visit to Windsor Castle, he encountered George the Third. The King noticed and spoke to Galt who, after the meeting, lingered in certain spots from which he might closely observe him. In this way "he caught a durable remembrance of his majesty's peculiarities and those traits of individuality" which reappear in Sir Andrew Wylie.[14] Three years after the Windsor Castle incident, Galt was presented at a levee, and, as he was making his bow, the King addressed him by name, though it was not customary for gentlemen to be announced in the drawing room.[15] It was not, however, wholly to Sir Andrew that he owed this special mark of recognition. His father, as he tells us, had done the King a special favour when they met somewhere overseas.

Galt owed a great deal to his acquaintance with the Blessingtons, the Countess in particular, and readily acknowledged his indebtedness when he wrote to her on July 27, 1822:

> ... somehow, since I have had the honour and pleasure of knowing you and my Lord so freely, I feel as if we were old friends; indeed, how can it be otherwise, for no other human beings ... have ever taken half so much interest in at once adding to my enjoyment and consideration. I am sensible of not only having acquired a vast accession of what the world calls advantages, but also friends who seem to understand me, and that too at a period when I regarded myself as in some degree quite alone, for all my early intimates were dead.[16]

Mrs. Galt's non-appearance at any of the Blessington functions should not be taken as evidence of her failure to match up in high society. The Countess's *salons* were, as a rule, reserved exclusively for men who shared her wide-ranging cultural interests or her advanced political views. Her circle, as Galt knew it, savoured greatly of the liberalism in politics that was coming to characterize the spirit of the age. Conspicuous at a later date in the upper class reformist coterie associated with the Blessington gatherings was the man who, when he went to Canada in 1838, was instrumental in re-shaping and re-directing its outdated system of government – John George Lambton, Earl of Durham, popularly known as "Radical Jack."

Galt may not have subscribed to Durham's political philosophy, but he claimed to have a special connection with Durham's great work in Canada, for, as he wrote to Mrs. Macnair, the wife of a Greenock banker, in 1838:

> I am not a little proud to think that even in my own time the prospective effects of my plans for the benefit of Canada are not ignored – a plan which I submitted in 1826, to the Government for the federal union of the American provinces is proposed by Lord Durham.[17]

Galt's name was ringing in London literary circles when the letter arrived from Canada that opened up a whole new prospect for him and eventually changed the entire course of his life. It was a long letter, dated at Niagara Falls, Upper Canada, December 1, 1820, and signed by Thomas Clark, Robert Grant and Robert Nichol. The substantive part of it read as follows:

Many of the inhabitants of this Province who sustained losses during the late War with the United States of America have regularly empowered us to apply to His Majesty's Government in their behalf, and to appoint one or more agents in England to manage their affairs –

Being satisfied of the justice of their Claims for Compensation, and of the expediency of interesting a person of experience to Advocate their cause, we have transmitted to our friends, Messrs. Gillespie, Gerrard and Co. of Gould Square [London] a full power for that purpose in which we have inserted your name.

It would have been gratifying to us to have had an opportunity of Communicating with you upon this subject and to have had your concurrence previous to transmitting the power had it been possible; but the time that has elapsed since the losses were sustained without fulfilling the Expectations of the sufferers, and their Actual Necessities at the present moment, rendering an immediate Appeal to His Majesty's Government in their behalf necessary left us no Option. We therefore hope that it may be Convenient for You to Afford us your Assistance in establishing their Claims –

The papers which are sent by this opportunity and which on Your Undertaking the Management of this business, will be Communicated to You by our friends, are we trust sufficiently Explicit to enable you to understand the Nature and Extent of the Claims.

Most of the Claimants are now in reduced circumstances from the effects of the War, and are unable to Make any pecuniary Advances to lower the expenses necessarily incident to the Solicitation and Management of their claims – We have therefore by a proper instrument obtained their sanction in retaining a Percentage on whatever Sum may be granted and paid over as a Compensation for the Same. –

Of this Commission (5 per cent) we are willing to relinquish three per cent as a Consideration for the aid which we hope to derive from you, and this is the only inducement we can hold out to You to assist us. –

Among the papers transmitted there is a letter from us to Lord Bathurst and a Petition to the House of Commons.

With respect to this last, we are of the Opinion that resort should only be had to it in the event of the failure of the direct Application to the Secretary of State . . .

In the event of Your undertaking this business we beg of you most distinctly to understand that having little experience in these Negotiations we implicitly rely on you and that we give you full power to withhold or amend whatever you may think fit.[18]

So far as we know, Galt had had no previous acquaintance with any of the three who signed the letter. They, for their part, as the letter indicates, had made no previous approach to him to sound him out on the business that they wished him to undertake.

Clark was born in Dumfries-shire, Scotland, in 1770, and got his start in Upper Canada as a clerical employee of the Honourable Robert Hamilton of Queenston who shared with the Honourable Richard Cartwright of Kingston the reputation of being among the commercial magnates of the day. As recompense, it is supposed, for conspicuous military service, Clark, who ranked colonel, acquired from the government the block of land which had been sold by Joseph Brant, the Mohawk chief, for the Six Nations Indians and which came to be known as Nichol township in the county of Wellington. The Clarks lived latterly at Clark Hill, an imposing house near Niagara Falls. Clark's name appears in the list of members of the Legislative Council of Upper Canada for 1791 – 1841.

Nichol, like Clark, a native of Dumfries-shire, was a lawyer in civil life, and some years after the War of 1812 was appointed Judge of the Surrogate Court for the Niagara district and Commissioner of Roads. His masterful direction of a flotilla for the transportation of reinforcements to the western front, during the war, earned him special recognition from Sir Isaac Brock, since it was largely instrumental in saving the day for the Canadians at Detroit. In something like record time Clark rose from command of a militia division to the rank of Quartermaster General. His estimated losses in private property as a result of the hostilities amounted to $27,000.

Grant is the most difficult of the three who signed the letter to Galt to account for. He may have been related to Nichol's wife, the grand-daughter of the Honourable Alexander Grant.[19]

The claimants' main concern was to secure Galt's services as their advocate with the government in London, for which, as merchant venturer, entrepreneur-at-large, and professional lobbyist, he would seem to them to be eminently qualified. It was, one gathers, with a certain zest that he undertook to act for the petitioners. The 3 per cent commission promised him on recovered claims was especially attractive, since he was "utterly bare" financially, as he told his father-in-law. He threw himself into the business on July 25, 1821, with a well researched statement of the case for the claimants addressed to the Lords of the Treasury.[20] Their response was "a very dignified evasion" of the issue.

Galt, however, was not to be so easily put off. He renewed his efforts to get through to the Treasury Department, not mincing matters and using every argument he could think of, "even to the contemplation of the colonists becoming rebels" if their just claims were not met. This frontal attack on the defenses of bureaucracy produced more positive results. An interview with Lord Liverpool, the Prime Minister, was suggested by Lord Bexley. There had at first been a prospect of Edward Ellice and Alexander Gillespie, a London merchant standing in as fully committed collaborators with Galt. Gillespie, however, withdrew and Ellice was willing to act only in an advisory capacity. At the beginning of March 1822 Galt, accompanied by Ellice, went to Fife House for the interview, at which Lord Bathurst, Secretary of State for War and the Colonies, and Lord Bexley were also present. An agreement was reached at this meeting that a loan should be raised to liquidate the claims, on the understanding that Galt was to raise the money,[21] but the agreement was knocked on the head when the Treasury insisted on advancing only half of the interest on the loan, and on the other half being put up by the Canadians.

A second proposal by the government to pay immediately a proportion of the claims at a rate of five shillings to the £, if Canada contributed the same amount, failed to materialize. It was then suggested that the government liquidate the claims, provided Upper Canada assumed responsibility for half of its own civil expenses. Galt was under the impression that an arrangement to that effect had been agreed to by Wilmot Horton, the Under-Secretary of State for War and the Colonies,[22] but, before that phase in his negotiations with the government was reached, he had decided to leave London. In the spring of 1823 he moved with his family to Scotland.

Chapter 4

THE PHILANTHROPIC DREAM[1]

"Being sick of a life of adventure," Galt informs us in the *Autobiography,* "and having before me only the education of my children, I resolved to remain in the neighbourhood of Edinburgh." The place of his choice was Eskgrove House which, with its grounds, adjoined the village of Eskgrove in the Lothians.[2] It was no great distance from Edinburgh and the town of Musselburgh was close by. In-laws of Galt's sister and relatives of his wife lived in the Edinburgh area.

Musselburgh was famous for its schools, and for Dr. David Macbeth Moir whose devotion to his patients was matched only by his devotion to literature. He and Galt became fast friends. There was also, as one of Galt's letters to Moir suggests, a special sort of friendly relationship between Moir and Galt's youngest son. Elizabeth Galt was in her element at Eskgrove which she wrote of as "a delightful place" and the boys were enrolled at the Musselburgh Grammar School which later numbered among its pupils George Brown, who was to become the Honourable George Brown of Upper Canada.

Early on the morning of December 16, 1823 Galt stood by the window of his study at Eskgrove. The world without lay white and silent, wrapped in its wintry sleep. The sky was dark and lowering. Would it snow again? He hoped not, if only for the sake of the visitor he was expecting from Upper Canada. As portrayed by his friend and near neighbour, Dr. Moir, Galt was then

> in his forty-fourth year, of Herculean frame and in the full vigour of health. His height might be about six feet one or two, and he evinced a tendency to corpulency. His hair, which was jet black, had not yet become grizzled; his eyes were small but piercing; his nose almost straight; long upper lip; . . . finely rounded chin . . . manly and strik-

ing countenance . . . Mr. Galt's manner [in conversation] was somewhat measured and solemn, yet full of animation, and characterized by a peculiar benignity and sweetness. Except when questioned, he was not particularly communicative; and in mixed company was silent and reserved.[3]

This was confirmed by Thomas Carlyle who after meeting Galt at a literary gathering in 1832 recorded that he "said little; but that little peaceable, clear and gutmüthig."[4] An old Irvine woman, with characteristic Ayrshire pithiness, described him as "a black-aviced (swarthy) man, wi' a loot (stoop) in the shoothers (shoulders), and geyly pockmarkit (very pockmarked)." The "loot in the shoothers" was also noted by Maginn in his comment on Maclise's drawing of Galt. As regards the old woman's last remark, McJannet mentions the unusual mortality in Irvine as the result of an epidemic of smallpox, and a nervous fever which made its appearance in 1755. The smallpox, he adds, was endemic in the town in the years 1781, 1784 and 1790.[5] According to a footnote to page 154 (verso) of the Pigott Papers, Galt's forehead was open and noble, with a suggestion of the cheerful social disposition by which he was characterized among his contemporaries. He impressed Samuel Strickland, when they first met in Upper Canada, as grave, dignified and prepossessing in appearance, naturally inclined to be kind and considerate, but at the same time commanding respect.

This pen portrait of Galt would not be quite complete without Katherine Thomson's observations on the man who awakened so many people's curiosity. Speaking of Galt as she knew him when he was living at London in Lindsay Row, she said:

When in the prime of manhood and the vigour of health he was an ungainly man: of height above the common, with a commonplace, though somewhat handsome caste of features . . . He spoke in a low monotonous voice . . . and he bent his high forehead down, and his eyes, long, narrow, and deep-sunk, were fixed steadily upon those of him to whom he addressed himself; and he went on, on, stopping at intervals to catch an exclamation from his listener, and to return it with his own dry laugh . . . He was then in the vigour of intellect and full of hope – that hope which circumstances so cruelly quenched. He was full of schemes – . . . ; and he had schemes without end . . . His mind was eager energetic and sanguine; his habits, without being exactly extravagant, were those of a man who abhors small calculations, whilst he is planning great schemes . . . He had a vast share of good humour; . . . a ready reply, a business-like precision, and the true Scotch hospitality . . . he enjoyed the eminence to which he had raised himself, but his was not the insolence of success, although it might be esteemed the elation of prosperity. His disposition was kind and cordial, and he appeared to feel a perfect reliance on the good will of those around him.[6]

Galt had stepped back from the window to stir up and put fresh fuel on the fire, when the door behind him opened to admit his visitor – Bishop Alexander Macdonell of the Glengarry settlement in Upper Canada, "an iron and devoted man in the tradition of those Catholic priests who had stood in line with the clansmen at Culloden,"[7] and a man too much overlooked where John Galt's coming to Canada and his connections, as well as those of his family, with the country are concerned.

Macdonell on his visit to Eskgrove House spent the whole day with Galt giving him all the information he required concerning the reserved lands of Upper and Lower Canada, which by a statute of 1791, had been set aside for the use of the Crown and the clergy in the proportion of one seventh of the land in every newly surveyed township to each of them. "From this circumstance," said Galt, "the Canada Company was ultimately formed."[8] According to G. J. Weir, Galt had already acquired some knowledge of how the waste lands might be used in the colonies from General Boyd for whom he acted as lobbyist in presenting his case to Parliament; but Macdonell's contribution was decisive.

While Macdonell was still with him Galt wrote to the Chancellor of the Exchequer stating that Macdonell possessed so much true information respecting Upper Canada that it would be useful in any future financial measures affecting the province, particularly in what might be required for the liquidation of the military claims, to confer with a person of Macdonell's knowledge and ability. Galt also expressed the hope that it would be seen that there was no lack of funds in the province to meet not only the claims of his clients but all the other civil expenses, if the reserved lands were properly made available. He had himself intended to address the Chancellor on the subject, and to suggest the expediency of appointing a commission to examine the state of the reserved lands, with a view to making them productive by sale to the treasury of the colony. However, Macdonell's arrival at Eskgrove on his way to London had made that unnecessary, as the information given by Macdonell would show that the war claimants might be indemnified without having recourse to any new taxes in the province. Galt at the same time provided Macdonell with a letter along much the same lines as the foregoing for delivery to Horton.

The earlier arrangement with Horton that the United Kingdom should undertake to discharge the war claims provided Upper Canada would be answerable for half of the civil expenses of the province no longer interested Galt. He had got hold of a new and better idea which emerged in the form of the plan he drafted on February 17, 1824, and submitted to Horton and the Chancellor of the Exchequer "for disposing of the *Reserved Crown Lands* in Canada in order to render the proceeds available for the discharge of *claimants,* the expense of making *canals* and *roads* and other extraordinary public demands and undertakings." This, however, did not prove acceptable because, like the proposals previously put forward for meeting the war claims, it laid responsibility on the government and involved a risk that the latter did not feel disposed to take.

It might look as if Galt had run out of suggestions, but in March, 1824, he came forward with a proposal of his own that a company be formed which would purchase the reserved lands in Upper Canada from the government and be prepared to clear and settle them. The new proposal was favourably received by the government, and by March 14, 1824, arrangements were in hand for the launching of the company. A first prospectus was issued and a provisional committee formed with the government's approval. Early in June a detailed statement of the terms on which the company would purchase the Crown lands was submitted to the government and more or less agreed to. When Galt put forward his proposal he recommended that, in connection with it, a public enquiry should be instituted, which he offered, if need be, to carry out himself.

Galt's first attempts to get indemnification for the war losses sustained by his Canadian "constituents" failed because, although the governments on both sides of the Atlantic were prepared to acknowledge the claims, neither had the money needed to indemnify the sufferers, owing to the effects in Britain and Canada of the depression that followed the Napoleonic War. His final attempt stood a much better chance of success because his proposal for the exploitation of the reserves in Upper Canada happened to fall into line with recent trends in Colonial Office policy regarding land disposal in Britain's overseas possessions. Galt's proposal could not but commend itself to Horton convinced as he was of the advisability and the desirability of putting the waste lands of the Crown overseas to work, thus relieving the treasury of responsibilities it was finding hard to meet. The changing climate of thought in the Colonial Office with regard to the waste lands in general, and, as exemplified in the case of the Canadas in particular, the disastrous consequences of the government's attempts so far to deal with them gave Galt his opportunity. His plan stressed the need for attracting "capitalists," people for whom the land they acquired by purchase would have a special vested interest. This, where other haphazard, makeshift expedients had failed, would be the key to its success. He would not be slow to impress on Horton the point made in the June 15, 1818, resolutions of the township representatives of the Midland districts of Upper Canada in their address to the Prince Regent, that there were millions of acres of fertile land in the country, on the credit of which, if put under proper management, vast sums might be raised for the improvement of the province and the eventual increase of revenue to Britain, without adding to the burden of taxation.

Galt's meeting with Macdonell and his own research into the resources of Upper Canada doubtless made him aware of the fact that the disposition of the reserved lands in the province and the uses to which they were put had given rise to grave economic problems and had become a breeding ground for political and ecclesiastical trouble. He pointed out to Horton that without some change in the situation, "the trade of the Canadians" could "never compete on equal terms with that of the Americans"[9] and that the reserving system ought not to be continued because, if persevered in, it would lead to endless controversies among the various priesthoods of the colony and cause the government much vexation.[10] The overall situation in the province in these and other respects is summed up by one writer as follows:

> The first practical problem ... was that of land settlement ... except in specially controlled districts like the Talbot settlement or Perth, Upper Canadian management exhibited all the mistakes that were possible. The normal procedure had been to grant 200 acres to each settler, at first free, later subject to fees which showed a tendency to rise; later still, quit-rents had to be paid and land bought in auction sales. Here as elsewhere regulations existed apparently in order that officials and politicians should break them. At first the districts settled were chequered with blocks not only of Clergy Reserves but also of Crown Reserves, in which lack of owners and cultivation held back the organization of the rest. Rules made in Britain were steadily disobeyed by colonial authorities; surveys were altogether inaccurate; vast grants were made to interested parties, some of whom were as remote from the scene as the Bishop of Quebec, and these swamped the little holdings of the genuine settler; unnecessary and heartless delays in the completion of formal grants drove immigrants in despair to practice 'squatting.' Lord Durham's *Report* condenses into a few figures the natural result: 'The area of the surveyed part of the province is stated to be 17,653,544 acres. Out of this there have been reserved for roads 450,000; for the clergy, 2,395,687; there have been granted and appropriated 13,660,838; and there remain to be

granted 1,147,019.' 'A very small proportion,' his Land Commission reported, 'perhaps less than a tenth, of the land thus granted has been even occupied by settlers, much less reclaimed and cultivated.'[11]

There was advance warning of other problems as well. On July 30, 1824, Sir Peregrine Maitland, the Lieutenant-Governor of Upper Canada wrote to Bathurst:

A report has lately come to us through private channels, that a joint Stock Company has been formed in England for the purchase and improvement of lands in Canada, and that the Government has actually transferred to them the whole of the Crown and two thirds of the Clergy Reserves . . . I hasten to avail myself of the earliest opportunity to offer to your Lordship two or three remarks, which if they have not already occurred, it may still not be too late to offer.

What, Maitland asked, of the settlers now in possession? What if they should find themselves at the mercy of private landlords who on the expiration of their present term would be able to bid against and buy them out? What of the clergy, the chief cause for concern? He was most anxious to ascertain that the reserves had not been disposed of, at a price very greatly below their worth. Many of the reserves located at a very early period, were now of great value. Closely related to the question of price was the maintenance of the Anglican establishment which "for various reasons, could never be safely, or properly, left dependent on the voluntary support of the people . . ."[12]

In spite of such problems, it was Galt's ambition that the Canada Company might have legislative influence in the province. On December 28, 1824 he wrote to Horton saying it would be in order to suggest to the Lieutenant-Governor the addition to the Legislative Council of someone intimately connected with the Company, and nominating himself as a candidate for the appointment. The Company, he argued in this letter, was "not necessarily precluded from legislative influence." Bathurst might be sounded out on the suggestion with a view to ascertaining "how far it might be advisable according to practical Constitutional principles for his Lordship to direct the adoption of the requisite measures for the attainment of that object." In his reply of January 6, 1825 Horton informed Galt that Simon McGillivray (who was made a Director of the Company) had approached Bathurst with an identical request. In due course Horton got in touch with Maitland to advise him that Galt's application for appointment to the Legislative Council which had been passed on to Bathurst, rested on Galt's claim of having initiated the Company, and that, the home government admitted, was advantageous to the province. A recommendation from Maitland would be needed, and to that extent the decision lay with him. If, Horton suggested, he felt there would be an objection to the appointment, he could easily point out to Galt some practical inconvenience to prevent his recommending it; if, on the other hand, no inconvenience was likely to arise, Bathurst on receipt of the recommendation would no doubt be disposed to ratify the appointment. There was, however, no recommendation.

Galt also wanted to see a union effected between the land granting offices in Upper Canada and the Canada Company, with the Crown assigning to the latter all the unappropriated lands, and the Company accounting for them to the Crown at a specific rate per acre, to be determined by periodic valuations at five or seven year intervals.[13] Nothing was done about this shrewd proposal when Galt advocated it. However, eighteen years later, subsequent to his death, Charles Widder who was then the land agent of the Company at Goderich, broached to Sir Charles Metcalfe, the Governor General, the idea that the Company be placed in control of all land transactions in the upper province, and in so doing, it has been said, "almost certainly pirated Galt's scheme"[14] – a further example of others reaping where Galt had sown.

While the final agreement between the government and the Company was being hammered out, Galt first saw the country of which he had frequently been reminded since he had first heard of Canada.

Horton had reservations about chartering the Company before an evaluation of the lands it proposed to purchase had been made by a commission. Commissioners accordingly were appointed – Galt and McGillivray representing the Company; Lieutenant-Colonel Francis Cockburn (senior member and permanent chairman of the commission) and Sir John Harvey who were empowered by Bathurst to act for the government; and John Davidson, a commissioner of Crown lands in Lower Canada, selected by Bathurst out of three candidates put forward by the Company. Their verdict was to be taken as final.

For the Atlantic crossing from Plymouth the Lords of the Admiralty directed that accommodation be provided on *H.M.S. Romney,* a fifty gun battleship recently fitted out for conveying government officials. During the voyage Sir John Harvey occupied himself with reading Galt's *Ringan Gilhaize,* a copy of which he had found on board. On February 25, 1825, after three weeks or thereabouts at sea, the Commissioners reached New York, and proceeded overland from there to Upper Canada.[15]

On arrival at York in March they received their commission under the great seal of the province from Sir Peregrine Maitland and prepared to go about their work. Galt was looking forward to a pleasant time at York. He seems to have regarded as a good augury of this, the attention given him by the press, of which he wrote in the *Autobiography:*

I had great reason to be personally obliged to the editors of some of the newspapers for their publications. Among others, I received a complete file of the Colonial Advocate. With the editor I was entirely unacquainted, and as little aware of the character of his politics. A file of newspapers, however, was a present that called at least for acknowledgement; but before sending my letter of thanks, which was written soon after I received the file, I turned the papers over cursorily, and here and there read a passage, which apprised me of the character of their politics, particularly a series of letters addressed to the attorney-general, . . . but I could not even acknowledge the present, without noticing the coarseness, in such a manner, however, as to convey my opinion with some delicacy; and as the paper evinced superior local information, I ordered it to be regularly sent to me.[16]

After several weeks of interviewing civil and military officers, as well as members of the provincial legislature then in session, holding meetings and studying charts, the Commission drew up a report. They left York on May 1, 1825, and early in June delivered their report to the Colonial Office in London. A dispute arose between the Canada Company and the government over the price decided on by the Commission for the lands being bid for by the Company, which the government felt to be too low; another between the government and the Church of England Clergy Corporation over management of the clergy reserves in Upper Canada. Contending that they were better qualified to administer these lands, the Clergy Corporation on March 24, 1825, petitioned the government opposing the sale of any of them to the Canada Company.[17] After protracted discussion an arrangement was reached whereby the proposal to include the clergy reserves in the deal with the Company was dropped, and the Company received by way of compensation 1,000,000 acres in one block in the Lake Huron area.

Early in the summer of 1826 Galt had a visit in London from Dr. John Rolph, a prominent member of the reform party in the Legislative Assembly of Upper Canada. A move was then afoot on the part of the legislature to enact a measure passed by the British government for conferring naturalization privileges on resident aliens, most of those so regarded being Americans who had settled in the province after 1783 and who now represented a large proportion of its inhabitants. Persons of this class already domiciled for seven years in the province were to be natural-ized immediately, others on completion of the seven years' residential requirement. All who applied for naturalization privileges and took an oath to renounce their American citizenship, were *ipso facto* to be regarded as British subjects. The reformist elements in the Upper Canada Assembly were opposed to the naturalization proposal because it assumed that American-born residents had no right to vote or hold office or even own property as they had been doing, without question, since they entered Canada.[18] Rolph was sent to London as the spokesman of the reformers, to negotiate better terms on the measure passed by the British government.

Rolph called on Galt to deliver a letter he had for him from the Honourable Thomas Clark.[19] Rolph had other letters for delivery in London and when Galt heard to whom they were addressed (Joseph Hume the left-wing politician being one of them) he prevailed on Rolph to hold the letters back till some other way of handling the situation could be found. Galt's solution was to take Rolph to see Horton at Downing Street. There and then a bargain was made with Rolph to the effect that if he withheld the "factious" letters he would be consulted about the provi-sions of the proposed naturalization bill. Shortly after that, Rolph showed Galt the draft of a bill which he had drawn up himself, but agreed, on Galt's advice, to suppress it in favour of the bill being framed by the Colonial Office which, according to the bargain made with Hor-ton, had taken Rolph into its confidence and had been given Rolph's promise of cooperation in return. When Rolph left for Canada he seemed perfectly satisfied with the arrangement that had been made.[20]

Galt had enough problems of his own without worrying about Rolph's. He was suffering from a mild recurrence of smallpox which had set in before he and the other commissioners began their work at York.[21] The strain of waiting to hear the outcome of the negotiations between the Company and the government was beginning to tell on him; and he had other worries – the "impending losses and embarrassments" that might arise from the circumstances which had befallen his interests in the shares of the Company;[22] and his mother, who was suffering the effects of a severe paralytic stroke that would bring about her death on July 18, 1826.

He had taken the liberty of impressing upon Bathurst that the with-holding of the Company's charter pending review of the price awarded for the lands in Upper Canada was having the effect of losing to the Company and Canada a good type of settler possessed of capital and get-ting a poor, destitute type instead. He also advised Bathurst that addi-tional expense to the tune of £1,000 had been incurred by the Company in consequence of the Commissioners being detained in London till the outcome of negotiations for a final settlement should be known, that the members of the Stock Exchange were withdrawing or asking their shares to be transferred, and that dissension had arisen among interested parties on the question of the separation of the clergy reserves from the Company's intended sphere of operation.[23]

His anxieties had not been lessened by a brush with the Admiralty over the Company's projected map of Upper Canada, copied from Lieutenant Bayfield's survey. The Commissioners of the Admiralty wrote Horton on September 5, 1825, pointing out that the *Courier* of the previous evening contained an advertisement intimating publication of the map (use of which Horton had requested). This seemed to disregard Bathurst's instructions that the map was not to be published or sold. Four days later Horton heard from the Commissioners again. Captain Parry, the Admiralty's hydrographer, and Lieutenant Bayfield had brought to their attention a mapseller's announcement in which both Bayfield and the Admiralty were named. They talked of bringing an injunction against the publisher. On expressing his willingness to leave out the names of Bayfield and the Admiralty, the publisher was, however, eventually given leave to sell the map,[24] which was apparently worked on by Galt's father-in-law and was to be dedicated, as Galt intended, to the King.

The Company was eventually launched on its career, with £1,000,000 of invested capital and responsibility for the settlement of 2,484,013 acres of land comprising 1,384,013 acres of Crown reserves, and, instead of the clergy reserves, the 1,000,000 acres (recently purchased by the government from the Chippewa Indians) in what came to be known as the Huron Tract, with 100,000 additional acres thrown in later to compensate for sandhills, rocks and swamps. The total cost was £344,375.7s.2d. sterling, at an average of 3s.6d. an acre, based on the estimated price of uncleared lands in Upper Canada prior to March 1, 1824 when the design of the proposed colony could not have been known in the province. In the Huron Tract the Company was authorized to apply a third of the purchase price to public works and improvements, and required over a sixteen year period to make payments to the provincial government of £20,000 for the first year and the last eight years, and from £15,000 to £19,000 per annum for the remainder. The Company also had the option of purchasing a certain amount of land over and above the acreage specified in the agreement. Galt was all along under the impression that the proceeds of the sale would be applied to liquidate the claims for war losses, but discovered, after the agreement had been reached, that the proceeds were to be appropriated to the use of the provincial government to pay for pensions and provide for the civil expenses of the province.[25]

At the first meeting of the Court of Directors of the Canada Company, which was held at the London Tavern late in July 1824, Galt was appointed to look after the company's interests in Canada with salary and expenses of £1,000 a year. John Biddulph, Richard Blanchard, Robert Downie, M. P., John Easthope, Edward Ellice, M. P., John Fullarton, Charles David Gordon, William Hibbert, Jr., John Hodgson, John Hullet, Hart Logan, John Masterman, Simon McGillivray, James McKillop, Martin Tucker Smith and Henry Usborne were on the Board of Directors; Charles Bosanquet was Chairman, William Williams, M. P., Deputy Chairman, and Thomas Smith, Accountant.

The chartering of the Company took longer than expected. Its charter, however, was passed on August 19, 1826. The Company was authorized by Act of Parliament "to purchase, take, hold, sell and dispose of lands, tenements and hereditaments situate" not only in Upper and Lower Canada but in Great Britain and Ireland or elsewhere in the British Dominions "which it may be necessary to acquire in order to the carrying the purposes of this charter into more complete effect."

The central feature of the Company's Arms, which stand at the head of the scroll containing John Galt's commission, is a shield, quartered, showing a plough; a sheaf of corn; a beaver; and, crossed, an axe and a cross-cut saw. The shield is surmounted by what looks like a maple in full leaf. The scroll beneath the shield has the inscription: *Non mutat solum genus* – "the soil does not change its nature."[26]

Attention had to be given to recruiting qualified personnel for service with the Company in Canada. In one of the Company's ledgers marked "Applications"[27] there are entries under the names of the Reverend John Strachan, Charles Prior, and Dr. William Dunlop. Strachan, Archdeacon of the Anglican church at York in Upper Canada, "offered himself to be of use to the Company," Mr. McGillivray one of the Company's directors, being of the opinion, it was noted, that Strachan "might be usefully employed perhaps under the name of a Commissioner allotting for his Department the signing of Deeds and Contracts and c." Prior was described as "accustomed to Land surveying, on a large scale and likewise to farming of all descriptions both scientific and practical." The entry for Dunlop contained the information that he was "desirous of an out of doors situation under the Company . . . assisted in the superintendence of making the Military Road between Lake Simcoe and Lake Huron [28] – was employed in directing the clearing of the Island of Saugur in the mouth of the Ganges in India," and was "a gentleman of good education and conduct" and "very highly connected in Scotland."

63

Prior and Dunlop were among the successful applicants for employment with the Company. On September 4, 1826 Galt intimated to Dunlop that by order of the Court of Directors he was appointed "Warden of the Company's Woods and Forests in Upper Canada." Dunlop was to be at hand to assist, and to act under orders from Galt, as laid down in the powers conferred on Galt by the Directors. Dunlop was instructed to go over the Company's lands, assess their value, decide which of them were fit to be sold immediately, and ascertain their adjacency to lakes, rivers, roads, settlements and mill sites. He was to gauge the quality and condition of the timber growing on the Company's property, find out where agricultural implements could be bought and at what price, obtain estimates and plans for the building of mills, blacksmith shops and inns, act as receiver of written applications for the purchase of lots, but make no binding agreements, and find out from those already settled on the land if it would be an inducement to immigrants to have part of the lots to be offered for sale cleared and some grain and potatoes planted in the spring in preparation for their arrival. Dunlop was restricted by his commission to collecting information, but he had authority to proceed against anyone who had cut down timber that belonged to the Company and to remove squatters unwilling to purchase land occupied by them. His salary would be at the rate of £500 a year, equivalent to the pay and allowances of an Infantry captain serving with the forces in Canada, and he was to proceed "with all practicable expedition" to the province of Upper Canada "and enter upon the duties of his office."[29]

The Court's instructions to Galt directed him, among other things to discover the best method of disposing, by public or private sale or both, of the Crown reserves, and the terms on which they should be sold; to obtain the fullest possible information regarding the Huron Tract, indicating the section he would recommend to the Directors and making such arrangements as he could with the provincial government for the layout of the Company's purchase; to look into the methods of established American land companies and record his findings in a journal to be sent to London, with a copy retained for the use of Company officials in Canada; to consider the most efficient way of managing the Company's business there, and to enlist any assistance considered necessary with "due regard to economy," all of which he was to report in due course to the London headquarters of the Company.[30]

Galt's commission required him to proceed to the Canadas to take up his duties "with all convenient dispatch." He had informed Horton that he intended going to Scotland a week later and sailing on October 1 either from the Clyde or Liverpool,[31] but subsequently changed his plans as shown by the following extract from a letter which his wife wrote to her aunt in Glasgow:

> I have been very unsettled since I saw you . . . Mr. Galt wrote me desiring me to remain into Edinburgh as he was to be in Scotland and did not wish to come to Musselburgh on account of the time which was taken going between it and Edin: accordingly I took lodgings there and after going in received a letter from Mr. Galt saying he can not leave London, . . . Mr. Galt is to sail for Canada the beginning of next month. John & Thom are placed at Dr. Valpy's School at Reading: they are very discontented and wish to be taken from the school . . . I suppose they are home sick . . . Mr. Galt thinks he will be absent 6 or 8 months and I must be very economical during his absence . . .[32]

With some justification Galt earlier gave vent to his feelings and told Horton that establishing the Canada Company had been the most vexatious, most profitless, most laborious business he ever engaged in, and that, no matter how much he got out of it, he could never be compensated for the domestic privations and other inconveniences he had been called on to endure;[33] and now, on the eve of his departure to take up his duties overseas, there were so many last minute things to be attended to that, as he said in a farewell note to Moir, he ran the risk of losing his passage. At last, feeling the full weight of the task ahead of him, yet confident that, if he did it well, he would receive "a degree of enviable credit," he boarded the *Brighton* at London for the crossing to New York.

Two incidents occurred before the ship was due to sail, that gave Galt much food for thought. When he called at the Colonial Office to say goodbye to Horton and collect a letter from the Secretary of State which he was to deliver on arrival at York in Upper Canada to Lieutenant-Governor Maitland, along with a despatch from the Directors of the Canada Company apprising Maitland of his mission, Horton advised him to ask Maitland, as a personal favour, to let him know if at any time a complaint was made against him.[34] Then, there was the communication Galt received from Archdeacon Strachan, who was at the time in Edinburgh, enclosing two letters which Strachan asked him to forward when he got to York, the one to the Attorney General, the other to Major Hillier, Maitland's secretary, and which, Strachan assured him, would help to make his situation in Upper Canada agreeable. Strachan's letter seemed friendly enough, but Galt got the impression (from the part of the letter that follows) that in Upper Canada he was already "viewed with jealousy and distrust."

I wish you to lay down as a principle never to be departed from that it is in the interest of the Canada Company to support the Colonial authorities and never to meddle in Colonial politics, for one side or the other you must by so doing offend, and so great and complicated are your interests that the determined enmity of any party would be productive of great loss.

On the whole, do not hesitate a moment in making the Attorney General and Major Hillier your advisers in all your plans, and confide in none else.

Converse with the Major oftener than write, and when to write is necessary prepare the draft with him before it is sent in officially.

Sir Peregrine is extremely nice in his writing, I might almost say fastidious, and therefore everything ought to be well weighed.

I can assure you the more confidence you put in those two gentlemen the better it will be for you, and the more satisfaction you will have in your mission . . .

I am sure you will take this letter in good part and see in it an anxiety to serve you, – the machine you have to conduct is complicated, and though your abilities are of a superior order I foresee that you will frequently require the assistance of me and my friends. But in order to receive that assistance, and indeed in order to enable us to give it, you must confide in us and in us only.[35]

By "me and my friends" Strachan meant the Family Compact in Upper Canada, whose only family ties were their "common vested interests, with, now and then, internal splutters of petty animosity,"[36] and who embodied a type of political mentality the genesis of which was "the conservative reaction from the French Revolution" that after 1815 "threw the British ruling classes into intense opposition to democracy."[37] As S. F. Wise has said,

Two streams of conservatism met and blended in the two generations of Upper Canadian history before the Union. One was that brought by the Loyalist founders of the Colony: an emotional compound of loyalty to King and Empire, antagonism to the United States, and an acute, if partisan sense of recent history. To the conservatism of the emigré was joined another, more sophisticated viewpoint, first brought by Simcoe and his entourage, and crystalized in the Constitutional Act of 1791: the Toryism of late eighteenth century England. What Upper Canada received from this source was not merely the somewhat creaking intellectual edifice of Blackstone and Warburton, but a conservatism freshly minted into a fighting

66

creed through Edmund Burke's philippics against the French revolution. The joining of two intensely counter-revolutionary outlooks in a colony as peculiarly situated as was Upper Canada had powerful consequences for the Canadian conservative tradition.[38]

The peculiar situation of Upper Canada, and its capital, York (the present-day Toronto) or "Little York," as it was called, was indeed one of the chief factors contributing to the preservation and the intensification of this conservative attitude. The province had something of the character of an island from its being hemmed in by the Ottawa and St. Lawrence rivers and the extensive chain of lakes.[39] In 1817 York "stood isolated in stretches of wilderness" and "though the seat of government, was still a small village of fewer than a thousand." [40]

Communication was slow and difficult, both within the province and with the outside world. Dunham remarks on the effect of this "in matters of greatest importance between Great Britain and Upper Canada."[41] The prevailing conservatism in such circumstances tended to become ultra-conservative and "formed a battle-ground on which were fought out the conflicting ideals of religion, education and government" as represented by the British and the American colonial points of view.[42] Yet, the Family Compact, while subscribing to the British viewpoint, were strangely ambivalent in their attitude to the British government. There was what has been referred to as "the determination of the Provincial Government to defend and enforce arbitrary principles, and to oppose the application and operation in the Province, of the acknowledged principles of the British constitution."[43] James A. Buchanan, the immigration agent for the British government at New York, asserted that Strachan and his protégé, John Beverley Robinson, had too long guided the destiny and dispensed the patronage of the province, and notwithstanding the opposition of persons and assembly had gone their way regardless of instructions from the Colonial Office. The springs of this attitude, however, were not simply political. "An innate fear of deterioration from their former moral and social standards breeds conservatism in the small minority of educated people, and in Upper Canada this class was conventional to the point of tyranny."[44]

It goes without saying that in a group of this sort nepotism would be rampant. The Family Compact had what has been called a monopoly on loyalty to its ruling principles, and amply rewarded such loyalty in appointments to office and the distribution of public land. Only those admitted to the "family" circle were considered respectable, and this was the class from which all appointments were made. The term "respectable" in this context has, of course, a special Family Compact connotation. Barnabas Bidwell, an exceptionally able and well educated man, was duly returned to the provincial legislature in the 1821 by-election for Lennox and Addington, yet because he was not acceptable to the official clique at York was afterwards expelled on a charge of being a person of immoral character and a fugitive from justice in his former domicile in the United States. Dr. William Warren Baldwin, "the only honest man in the province," was disbarred from election for his known reformist sympathies.[45]

Such was the Government House party, as it was known in Upper Canada, and of which Lord Durham wrote:

> For a long time, this body of men, receiving at times accessions to its numbers, possessed all the highest public offices, by means of which, and of its influence in the executive council, it wielded all the powers of government; it maintained influence in the legislature by means of its predominance in the legislative council; and it disposed of a large number of petty posts which are in the patronage of the government all over the province. Successive governors as they came in their turn, are said to have either submitted quietly to its influence, or, after a short and unavailing struggle, to have yielded to this well-organized party the conduct of affairs. The bench, the magistracy, the high offices of the Episcopal Church, and a great part of the legal profession, are filled by the adherents of this party: by grant or purchase they have acquired nearly the whole of the waste lands of the province; they are all-powerful in the chartered banks, and, till lately, shared among themselves almost exclusively all offices of trust and profit. The bulk of this party consists, for the most part, of native-born inhabitants of the colony, or emigrants who have settled in it before the last war with the United States; the principal members of it belong to the Church of England, and the maintenance of the claims of that Church, has always been one of its distinguishing characteristics.[46]

In any condensed account, such as is here being presented to the reader, of what the Family Compact stood for over a long period of its existence, one is apt to lose sight of its varying aspects at different stages of its history, some better and some worse. One of the worst aspects it ever presented to the world was during the years from 1815 to 1837 when the "changing but growing 'council crowd' " was led by Strachan and Robinson and "developed its perverted form under the influence of Sir Peregrine and Lady Sarah Maitland."[47]

The personal element played an important part in provincial politics which "developed through phases determined as much by political opinion in the province as by the character of the existing Lieutenant-Governor."[48] Perhaps there never has been a Lieutenant Governor whose character so much determined the situation and the outlook of officialdom in the province as Sir Peregrine Maitland who owed his appointment to Lord Bathurst and held office from 1818 – 1828. Born in Hampshire, England in 1777, he entered the British army as an ensign in the Foot Guards in 1792, and was on active service throughout the Napoleonic Wars, being in command of the first brigade of the first division at the battle of Waterloo. He was created K. C. B. in 1815 and married Sarah, daughter of the Duke of Richmond and Lennox. Maitland has been described as "tall and stately, of sad pensive aspect, and very reserved in manner." One wonders what sort of a match he would be for Strachan whose ecclesiastical countenance, with the firm set mouth drooping slightly at the corners, and the hard, cold, somewhat proudly disdainful eyes, has the glintiness of the granite quarried near his native Aberdeen.[49] From the owner of that face one would, at least, know what to expect, whereas the Lieutenant-Governor's sad pensive aspect was a mask concealing the real man, who ruled, "in spite of legal technicalities, at his little capital, York, as a despot limited only by inexperience and the British Parliament," who had neither "flexibility of mind" nor "power of resisting prejudice," and "little interest in seeing that justice was impartially administered" where political opponents were concerned.[50]

The following abridged account of his administration, published in 1841, should enable the modern reader to form an estimate of the far from salutary influence exerted on the destinies of Upper Canada during Maitland's term of office as Lieutenant-Governor:

When Sir Peregrine succeeded Gov. Gore, great hopes were entertained from the conciliatory nature of his instructions, that every grievance would be adjusted and a better policy pursued: but the issue of his administration proved more restrictive and intolerable than any former one . . .

This cursed faction, instead of meeting the punishment due their crimes, have been raised, at every immolation, to higher honours, and in every case they have been promoted in direct opposition to the complaints of the people . . .

Sir George Murray, then principal Secretary of State for the Colonies, . . . rebuked Sir P. Maitland for his long and artful despatch against the Assembly's parliamentary privileges. Yet he was permitted, without further censure, to follow his old course.

The people petitioned his Majesty's Government, to recall this pious Nero, and strongly urged them to consider their deplorable condition, and afford that relief which the exigency of their sufferings, and the peculiar situation of their affairs demanded . . . But instead thereof, the withering and oppressive system pursued by the Administration, had rendered unavailing the natural resources and advantages of the country, and paralyzed all its enterprise.[51]

The challenge facing Maitland when he took up duty as Lieutenant-Governor in August, 1818, was to "improve the system of land administration, including that of the Reserves, or face further legislative pressures."[52] It is true that there was widespread popular indifference to the protocol of such things, the people being more concerned about ploughs than they were about politics. Those in power nevertheless had a responsibility to see that pressing reforms and needed improvements were brought about. "After the battle of Waterloo, the Armageddon of the old world," Galt wrote in *The Literary Life,* "the result I apprehended took place. Peace brought calamities, in so much that even statesmen openly confessed that the 'revulsion' puzzled their science." They at least recognized the cause, and their puzzlement was proof of their concern to discover the remedy. Maitland, a true-blue Tory of the most reactionary type, was not much given to soul-searching of that sort. "He had a soldier's idea of discipline and authority, . . . his language and bearing were resented by civilians," and he openly showed his contempt for the members of the provincial Assembly who, whenever they displeased him, felt the sharp edge of his tongue.[53] He fervently believed that the suppression of liberal opinion in any shape or form was the all important aim, and was prepared to go almost any length in his zeal for achieving it, as when he "spent large sums of public money in placing poor settlers upon lands sold to them on credit" to secure their loyalty to the reactionary cause and use them as a foil against the forces of democracy.[54]

In that respect his sentiments were no different from those of other occupants of the Lieutenant-Governorship. True to the spirit of the late eighteenth century brand of English Toryism he professed, Simcoe (1791 – 1796) in a letter of December 30, 1790 to the Archbishop of Canterbury wrote in reference to Upper Canada that every establishment that upheld the distinction of ranks, and decreased the undue weight of the democratic influence ought to be introduced. Sir John Colborne (1829 – 1836) maintained that "democracy was the curse of the colony" and that "all concessions to popular demands should be denied,"[55] while Sir Francis Bond Head (1835-1838) decided at the outset of his career that "democracy was the foe against which it was his mission to contend." [56]

The means employed by Maitland to gain his ends may at times have been dubious, but his motive was always clear. The same cannot be said unequivocally of his opponents whose fulminations against his administration and against him personally were apt to convey the impression that the reformers were activated by only altruistic principles. The motives of many who marched under the banner of reform were, however, not as pure as they seemed to be. In the battle that raged round the proposal to naturalize resident aliens, for example, vested interests in land underlay much of the oratory on the inalienable rights of man.

As for Strachan, through Robinson and others who adhered to his unbending Toryism, he aimed at acquiring in the provincial government "a growing influence such as no other person" could "possess and the means of communication which would be much increased" had he the decision-making power in certain areas.[57] His eventual acquisition of influence very much akin to this was not entirely due to scheming or conniving on his part. In the existing machinery of government there were patent weaknesses which played into his hand and perhaps made it inevitable that anyone possessed of his tenacity of purpose should find himself in a position to shape the course of events. Often for various reasons there were not sufficient members present at the meetings of either the Executive Council or the Legislative Council to form a quorum (three members in the one, and the Speaker plus three members in the other). There were actually two sessions during which most of the business of each of these two bodies was transacted by three of its number. Strachan at times was the only one who turned up at the Legislative Council and "on these occasions the venerable gentleman, with all due solemnity, formally adjourned the meeting."[58] Religious practices, as approved by the Family Compact, and their particular brand of politics were one and indivisible. Maitland was not the only Lieutenant-Governor of Upper Canada who believed that the promotion of the Church of England was an essential part of his governmental responsibilities. The members of the governing clique at York, drawn from the ranks of the Church of England, carried their political intolerance into the religious life of the province, taking it upon themselves to pass disabling legislation against both ministers and people of other religious persuasions. Strachan, the presiding genius of this provincial oligarchy, doctored the statistics in the religious chart (a census of religious denominations in the province) which he drew up in 1827, to make it appear as if the Anglicans were in the majority, "which," as has been said, "marks the zero point of Canadian ecclesiastical honesty."[59] Though the clergy reserves had been set aside for the benefit of all Protestant denominations, Strachan fought tooth and nail to manoeuvre

71

them into the sole possession and control of the Anglican party.

Sir George Arthur who was Lieutenant-Governor from 1838-1841 let it be plainly known how he felt about such things when he wrote:

> The more I have considered the Clergy Reserves question, the more I regret and mourn over the past proceedings of the members of the Church of England . . . One of the most unhappy . . . occurrences in this Province appears to me to have been the elevation of a native of Scotland over the Church of England. Doctor Strachan, I have no doubt, possesses many of the enviable qualities you assign to Him and I do not question He is much looked up to amongst a certain class; but even by many members of his own Church and by many Ministers of it, I have found ever since I came Here that his dominion has been very far from being acceptable.[60]

Public education was regarded by the Family Compact as one of its special preserves. The Compact established a grammar school in each district at public cost but divorced from public control, and charged tuition fees that only they or others equally well off could afford. By Strachan's persistent efforts King's College was founded as an exclusively Anglican establishment at Toronto in 1825. Two years later it was endowed "with 225,000 acres of School Lands, and an appropriation of £1,000 a year for sixteen years from the proceeds of Crown Reserves sold to the Canada Company." Concern was felt at the Colonial Office about the tests that those put in charge of the college were required to undergo in order to establish the orthodoxy of their religious views. The efforts of the reformers to get the Legislative Council to remedy this anomalous situation failed repeatedly, because the Council was dominated by Strachan and six of his former pupils.[61] The situation in Upper Canada before Galt arrived to take up his duties for the Canada Company at York was, as has been said, "nothing but a mixture of unhappy circumstances." The scene was already set for the drama which, before it was played out, was to end for him in bitter disappointment and inescapable tragedy.

Chapter 5

BEYOND THE WASTE OF SEAS[1]

On November 23, 1826 Galt notified the Directors that, after a rough and disagreeable passage of thirty-four days, he had landed at New York where he was greeted with the encouraging news from Upper Canada that reports of the final establishment of the Canada Company had given a boost to the value of its land. He was also greeted with news of a less encouraging nature concerning William Lyon Mackenzie, the proprietor and editor of the *Colonial Advocate* which on May 18, 1824 made its début at Queenston. (Later that same year the paper was moved to York.) From the moment the paper appeared it was used as the vehicle for Mackenzie's outspoken criticism of the Maitland administration in general and of Maitland in particular. On the evening of June 8, 1826 a band of young men in the civil service, including Maitland's private secretary, broke into Mackenzie's premises in his absence and wrecked his printing-press. Mackenzie filed suit for £2,000 and was awarded £625 in damages, having produced in his defense, while the claim was being heard, Galt's written acknowledgement of the complimentary file of the newspaper which Mackenzie had sent to him.

According to his instructions Galt went forward from New York to investigate the practices and procedures of two of the best known and most reliable land investment corporations in the United States, the Pulteney Company at Geneva and the Holland Company at Batavia. He also picked up useful information from private sources and received some assistance from the United States land offices. His visits to the Pulteney and Holland Companies enabled him to see what was best in their systems and what was capable of improvement as well as defects he should avoid in working out a system for the Canada Company.[2]

After completing his investigations he set out for York via Buffalo and

Niagara. When he got to the latter on December 10 he wrote to Mackenzie as follows:

Sir,

On my arrival in America, I heard, with extreme surprise, that you had produced in a late action for damages, a letter from me, commending the manner in which you conducted the *Colonial Advocate.*

You had, Sir, the courtesy, when I was last in the Province, to send me a file of your Paper, and I returned of course a civil note for the present – the contents of that note I do not recollect, but as my political sentiments differ from yours, I cannot conceive how any expression of mine, even complimentary to your talents, could imply that I approved of the style and temper of the *Colonial Advocate.*

As I wish my political opinions not to be misunderstood, I should be obliged to you to publish this, together with the letter produced in Court.[3]

There is nothing to indicate that Mackenzie made any move to comply with Galt's request. Even if he had, it would not have made much difference. The damage had been done; the fat was already in the fire.

Another shock awaited Galt before he reached his destination. He happened to pick up some Canadian newspapers containing the report of the speech delivered by Lieutenant-Governor Maitland at the opening of the provincial parliament and discovered to his astonishment that Rolph had given notice of his intention to bring in his own alien bill, even though the Governor had announced a similar measure in his speech-from-the-throne. The way in which Rolph had acted was, for Galt, "a prostration of principle" the like of which he had never experienced on the part of any man. He reached York on December 12 and went immediately to present to Maitland the documents with which he had been entrusted on leaving England by the Directors of the Canada Company and the Secretary of State. He also handed over the two letters Strachan had asked him to deliver. While in conversation with Maitland he complained of Rolph's behaviour and said that if Rolph did not desist he would feel duty bound to petition the lower house against the "nonsensical bill" as hostile to the well-being of the province, and as such indirectly injurious to the interests of the Canada Company. Then he mentioned the advice given him by Horton that if at any time a complaint was made against him he should ask Maitland, as a personal favour, to let him know of it himself. Maitland readily obliged by drawing attention to the letter Galt had written to Mackenzie and the latter's use of it at the trial for damages in connection with the raid on his printing press. Maitland, however, politely invited Galt to have dinner at Government House.

In the meantime Galt sent for Rolph and, in the presence of a witness, reproached him for what he had done. Rolph lamely excused himself and offered, one can only think cynically or facetiously, to introduce Galt to some of the members of his faction. Galt told Rolph that he wanted nothing to do with him or them, and "never afterwards spoke to him or in any way recognized him, further than once in passing on the highway by a cold bow."[4] By the time he had dealt with Rolph he was due at Government House for the dinner to which he had been invited. While there he thought he perceived "some sort of free-masonry" between Major Hillier and the Attorney General suggesting that they seemed not to have previously communicated with each other, and had something to say together. He got into conversation with them and mentioned his surprise at the way in which Rolph had acted, reaffirming his intention of exposing Rolph by petition if he persisted in his efforts to force his alien bill. Neither Hillier nor the Attorney General gave any indication of having received the letters which Galt had transmitted on Strachan's behalf.[5]

Maitland's first salvo about Galt's involvement with Mackenzie was mild compared to what followed and for which, on his own confession, Galt was not wholly unprepared. He had an "inexplicable boding of evil" when he entered Upper Canada and it seemed to take tangible form in the shape of the letter he received from Maitland on December 13, the day after the dinner party at Government House. The coldly formal nature of the letter could not conceal Maitland's indignation, and a glance was sufficient to let Galt see Maitland's reason for writing it. Hillier had reported what Galt had said the previous evening about Rolph. The real sting of the letter was in the last paragraph where it was very plainly stated that it was only by Galt's abstaining altogether from mixing in local politics that a good understanding could be insured; for, as Maitland frankly confessed, the impressions he had received from past occurrences would be very apt to dispose him to put an unfavourable construction upon such interference. Galt sent a note to Hillier on December 14, in which he said that he surely must have made himself "confusedly understood" the other evening. He was utterly unable to comprehend how any remonstrance with Mr. Rolph to mitigate the virulence of party animadversion should have led to the mistake of supposing he was "courting the opposition." Hillier's answer came back immediately. He was not aware, he told Galt, of having misunderstood him, because Galt had certainly admitted to having already sent for a member of the Assembly to remonstrate with him on the subject of a measure introduced by the latter into the House as being at variance with a previous understanding reached between them in London and that they were to see each other again about it. This, Hillier thought, was not incorrectly designated courting the opposition, for the gentleman Galt was in communication with was generally regarded as one of the leaders of a party in the Assembly upon most occasions opposed to the measures of the government.[6]

The matter might have been let go at that if Galt's reply had been only the apology that it set out to be, but it tended, as it went on, to prolong the agony by harping somewhat petulantly on the impressions from past occurrences which Maitland claimed to have received. Maitland asserted that Galt, on his previous visit to the province had been specially sought out by persons professing that they had rights to claim and wrongs to redress, and that he had given the appearance of interposing, and of having every right to interpose, in the public affairs of the colony. Letters went back and forth between Galt and Maitland daily till the correspondence ended on December 16 with Galt's note to Maitland enclosing a copy of the report he was sending to Horton on the whole Mackenzie/Rolph affair.[7] Galt, does not appear to have realized the unwisdom of keeping up the argument, nor how sensitive an issue the Rolph incident had become where Maitland was concerned. Maitland was strongly in favour of excluding aliens from the Legislative Assembly. Rolph was the acknowledged champion of the anti-alienists, a rising member of the growing opposition which two years later would topple Maitland from his pinnacle, and, as he has been described, one of "the true predecessors of the rebels of '37."[8] In his report of December 18, 1826 to Horton, Galt said that his reception by Maitland had been most satisfactory but that he was bitterly disappointed by the outcome of his efforts to moderate party animosity in Upper Canada in the interests of the Canada Company, which were bound to be impaired by whatever tended at a distance to exhibit the country in an unsettled or unsound state. Although it was not to be supposed that the Hillier report was intended to misrepresent him to Maitland, it seemed to have left a most unfavourable impression. The mistake which had been made in confusing the hopes which he (Galt) had been led to entertain of more moderate proceedings on Rolph's part with the measure brought forward by Rolph in violation of parliamentary decorum, had been pointed out to Hillier. There was nothing, however, to reflect other than honour on the candour and the feelings of the Lieutenant-Governor.

Galt could not understand what Maitland meant by saying that he tried to extend unduly his enquiries as a commissioner. If receiving visits of civility from some of the Canadian war claimants was imputed as a fault, he must certainly plead guilty, but he could not think of anything he had done that could be seriously construed as interposing in public affairs or viewed as "colonial treasons." It would be seen from the letter addressed to Mackenzie, which he had asked to be published with some comments regarding the circumstances under which it had been written in the *Upper Canada Gazette,* that he was trying to be civil. Because he did not approve of Mackenzie's virulence, he had confined himself to praising in the abstract the freedom of speech exhibited by the *Colonial Advocate.* The letter, and a note ordering a subscription of the *Colonial Advocate* for the Company comprised all the correspondence that had ever passed between Mackenzie and himself. In subscribing to the *Colonial Advocate* on behalf of the Company, no special patronage was involved, as he wanted all the provincial newspapers to be ordered for the Company's office in London. It was a long time since he had started to take an interest in the prosperity of the province. He was the originator and organizer of the Canada Company, and the person through whose connections to begin with the capital was raised. That was sufficient to assure the Lieutenant-Governor that the peace and progress of the colony could have no enemy in him. He had done nothing for which he needed to be pardoned, could not go back on anything he had said and did not wish one word that he had written to be erased.[9] There was no reason he could see for conducting himself according to any other rules than those that had placed him in the trust he exercised, and he was happy to have the word of the Lieutenant Governor that he would put nothing in the way of that trust being carried out.

In that letter to Mackenzie (dated at York, March 28, 1825) Galt had succeeded in being civil, but some of the things he wrote went beyond mere civilities, and one can readily imagine how they were likely to affect and offend anyone of the Family Company mentality. In colonies and places remote from supreme government, the letter stated, people in public trust were "apt to consider themselves as parts of that great abstraction *Government,* and to mistake attacks on their own conduct as factious and seditious movements," while "the motions and machinery of Government being in a much smaller compass" were "seen more in detail than at home," and, as a result, "the workings of personal feeling" were "apt to excite a more acute invidiousness." The letter ended by assuring Mackenzie that he could have no better task than upholding the frank courageous spirit of independence among a remote people.[10]

Maitland's comment on Galt's previous visit to the province seems to have particularly nettled Galt. In rebuttal of Maitland's allegation he contended that if anything was known of him personally, it would not have led to the suspicion that he would turn the influences of a great trust, held only for a limited time, to dealing in a small way with provincial discontents. In support of his contention he also gave in the *Autobiography* a list of the people who, during his previous visit to the province, called at the headquarters of the commissioners in York, and whose business, he pointed out, was as much with the other commissioners as with him. The list included the following: Major Hillier, a judge, the Solicitor General, the Chief Justice, the Attorney General (whom, as Galt elsewhere informs us, he chose as his legal adviser), Mr. D. Boulton, Mr. George Hamilton, M. P. P., the Speaker, Mr. Rolph and two gentlemen, the Inspector General, the Surveyor General, Colonel Fitzgibbon, Judge Boulton, Captain Brown an officer of the garrison, a gentleman (Dr. Baldwin, Galt thought), and the Honourable T. Dickson. All of these, Galt explained, were visits of ceremony. Colonel T. Clark was often there, and John Brant the Indian chief dined with him one day at the commissioners' mess.[11]

It is hard to see how Galt could have expected to vindicate himself, at least in Maitland's eyes, by reference to a list containing the names of Rolph and Baldwin, for the simple reason that they were actively opposed to the Maitland administration.

Galt registered the Company's charter at York, then proceeded for the same purpose to Quebec in January 1827. He was joined there by Dunlop who had arrived in Upper Canada a month ahead of him. In his inspection of the Company's lands in the eastern and Ottawa districts Dunlop had run into the first snag. The surveys were overgrown or had never been completed and lots often could not be located. To deal with this surveyors would have to be hired, and expenses incurred for which no provision had been made. Commitments of that kind could not be taken on without authority, so Dunlop had decided to let them wait till Galt got to Upper Canada.

The warmth of the welcome Galt received at Quebec from the Earl of Dalhousie, the Governor General, may have encouraged him to think that there might still be some chance of getting the claims of the war sufferers met, but Dalhousie regarded it as a rather hopeless task. Nevertheless, Galt felt that in the lower province a better understanding existed regarding him than in Upper Canada. For variety and enjoyment he considered the month spent at Quebec as the best in his whole life. The city was full of Highland regiments, he told Moir when he wrote him on February 22, 1827 giving him all the latest news. No bounds were set to the hospitality of the gentlemen to whom Galt was introduced. There were endless private parties, and an amateur theatre was got up for which Galt wrote a farce entitled "Visitors, or a Trip to Quebec." The Earl and Countess of Dalhousie attended the performance from the proceeds of which £50 were donated to the Emigrant Society, with the balance applied to defraying the cost of fitting up the theatre. Several years later Galt expressed his lasting gratitude for the kindness Dalhousie had shown him during the Quebec visit in the following lines:

His hapless songs, the restless bird,
That's cag'd afar from woodland bowers,
For pastime sings, heard or unheard,
To wile away the weary hours;
So are my chamber'd moments spent,
Dalhousie, of an auld descent.

Embalm'd by gratitude, entire,
I still remembrances behold, –
When Hope, all-shivering, needed fire,
And warm'd, resolv'd to face the cold;
Cheer'd by the shelter then bestow'd,
I dar'd a dark and drifted road.

The worth of gift or grant, my Lord,
Can ne'er in sterling well be known:
The value of the heart'ning word
Is in the kindness of the tone.
Thus feeling made the widow's mite
A pearl in the appraiser's sight.[12]

While at Quebec Galt also took part in the proceedings of an agricultural society, and fell to speculating on the St. Lawrence River's navigational possibilities. It did not seem to him far-fetched to imagine that the time would soon come when the St. Lawrence below Quebec would be made navigable all winter; there was no disputing the fact that the river's tidal currents were open, but there was nothing to hinder "judicious art" from attempting to overcome what at that time was regarded as an insurmountable obstacle. As he sat, wrapped in furs, in the sleigh on the return journey to York, his mind was at work on other schemes of the same sort – "the practicability," as suggested by Dunlop, "of rendering the Petite Nation river navigable" so as to make it the course for a canal leading into the Ottawa. Galt even proposed the formation of a joint stock company to carry the suggestion into effect from the standpoint of its value as a public utility, but in putting the proposal forward he had other things in view. It was essential to the prosperity of the Canada Company to make the country better known and to hold out inducements to emigrants to locate on the Company's property, which, as he saw the situation, could be best achieved by assuring them of employment when they arrived; and that, he reckoned, could be provided by setting a price on certain lots of Company land and taking work by emigrants on the canal project in lieu of payment. As Katherine Thomson, already quoted, said of him, he was full of schemes and had schemes without end.

Galt was not much impressed by York for he called it "one of the vilest blue-devil haunts on the face of the earth."[13] It stood on the shore of Lake Ontario, almost level with the lake. The low lying, swampy land in its immediate vicinity made it "better calculated for a frog-pond or beaver-meadow than for the residence of human beings."[14] When the site of the town was selected in 1793 it was occupied by one wigwam. In 1825 it had 1,336 inhabitants and 250 houses including the residence of the Lieutenant-Governor, as well as Methodist, Presbyterian, Roman Catholic and Anglican places of worship, the last named being under the pastoral care of the Reverend John Strachan. Streets had by that time been regularly laid out, but only partially completed "and in wet weather the unfinished streets" were "if possible, muddier and dirtier than those of Kingston."[15] From this it can be readily appreciated how the capital of Upper Canada came to be known as "Muddy York."

As soon as Galt returned from his Quebec visit to these none too enlivening surroundings, his work began in earnest. There were between two and three hundred offers to purchase lots of land waiting to be dealt with, which, added to the task of "establishing a system and routine for the future management of the Company's affairs," much exceeded the responsibilities which, on leaving England, he had agreed to undertake. His mission, as then stipulated, was to be one of enquiry only, and he had eight months to carry it out. On December 28 he wrote to Canada House (the London headquarters of the Company at 13 St. Helen's Place) pointing out that he was pressed with business which he was not yet in a position to take in hand on a regular basis. He asked for an extension of time on his appointment as superintendent, a request which was acceded to eventually, and in the meantime went ahead with the business requiring immediate attention.

Finding suitable working accommodation in such a place as York was something of a problem, but Galt managed to secure as an office, at a rent of $1.00 a week, a room about ten feet square. He made his living quarters in the Steamboat Hotel. The hotel got its name from "the spirited delineation of a steam-packet of vast dimensions, extending the whole length of the building, just over the upper verandah."[16] Galt described it as "a mean, two storey house." It stood in the market block, near the centre of the Front Street area opposite the harbour. "The reader," as Galt wrote in the *Autobiography,* "is probably acquainted with the manner of living in the American hotels, but without experience he can have no right notion of what in those days was the condition of the best tavern in York . . . being constructed of wood, every noise in it resounded from roof to foundation." One morning, as Galt sat at breakfast the sounds of an Irish wake in full swing could be heard on the premises. Outside, the croaking of the frogs from time to time was apt to give the impression that the capital of Upper Canada was, indeed, better suited for a frog-pond than for a human habitation. Feeding time in the Steamboat was, according to local custom, at two in the afternoon. This did not suit Galt with his "genteel boarder" point of view, so he dined in the evening by himself. His "natural disposition to sequestration," as he called it, was attributed to pride and "undervaluing those among whom it was" his "destiny to sojourn." He was called "Captain Grand" and was in fact so represented in a not unfriendly biographical sketch of him which appeared in print while he was a guest of the hotel.

Once all the "indispensable domestic and official arrangements" were duly attended to, Galt applied himself to collecting information so as to begin clearing the ground for his colonizing operations. He was soon convinced that the only system then existing in the province was the system which individual settlers, owing to their original poverty, had had no choice but to adopt.[17] Permission was granted by the Directors of the Company to attempt a settlement, so Galt proceeded to direct the inspection of a block of the Company's land some forty thousand acres in extent, with a view to finding a suitable situation for a town. All the reports sent in to him recommended the spot where Guelph now stands.

On February 26, 1827, while on the way to Cornwall, he answered a letter from the Directors, which he had received five days earlier. He broached the possibility of their authorizing a liberal subscription to the Society for the relief of Emigrants at Quebec, on the ground that a few hundred pounds given to it occasionally would bespeak the goodwill of the Canadian people toward the Company. He also suggested the making of locks on the River Ouse or Grand to render it navigable. He was preparing a prospectus on Company holdings, he informed the Directors, and was anxious to have agents appointed as soon as possible at New York and Quebec. Plans for an expedition to Lake Huron, with Dunlop at the head of the exploring party, were in hand. In the light of Dunlop's investigations he foresaw some very delicate business. Errors had been found in concession lines, landmarks were obliterated, and many of the lots allocated to the Company were already occupied, with valid title to possession, while others had been withheld. He was, however, assured of the Governor's desire to render his task easy and, if an example could be set by certain prospective settlers of good name and family, such as the son of Lord Alloway and Mr. Alex. Dunlop of Edinburgh, things would go very well.[18]

Reporting further on March 14, from York he stated that farmers could, at no great cost, be enlisted to help with roadmaking, that the construction of canals was contemplated, and that surveys had been taken. He had found when he arrived that many persons in the province desired to purchase the Crown reserves contiguous with their farms for their children and relatives. From this class of people, some of whom urged their claim to a preference so strongly that it would not be judicious to refuse, he had had 370 offers besides those made to Dunlop.

On March 19, Galt wrote from York to Dunlop advising him that, as the business of the Company called him away and he might be out of touch with him for some weeks, he was leaving certain instructions for him while he was away or until such time as he might instruct him to the contrary. Dunlop was to proceed the following day to Ancaster to inform Charles Prior, the overseer of the Guelph operations, of his arrival and receive whatever information had been collected concerning the Guelph block, additional to or explanatory of the regular report a copy of which was subjoined. Dunlop was then to proceed with Prior and two other employees of the company to the proposed site of the city of Guelph. He was to examine the site carefully and *diligently* and if it appeared to be inconvenient or ineligible, he was to make a tour of the Guelph block for the purpose of selecting a place better adapted for the offices and public buildings of the Company; but if it appeared that the proposed site was well fitted for such purposes, no time was to be lost in making arrangements for procuring building materials. Because it was absolutely essential that a road should be cut into the block as a preliminary step to any permanent improvement, Dunlop was to make a careful examination of the country between the settled parts of the townships bordering on the Company's lands and run a blaze between these and the Company's boundary on the line which could be cut with the least expense to the Company, but after passing the Company's limits he was to run the road along the most convenient line that the general face of the country pointed out without having any reference to straight lines and angles.

Having set the business of the Guelph block in train Dunlop was then to explore the Huron territory. In all measures undertaken by him for that purpose, the proper course for him would be to take the advice or at least ascertain the opinion of Mr. Dickson and other intelligent gentlemen and persons in the neighbourhood whose practical experience might be of value to the Company. During his absence in the woods he was to report his proceedings and forward to Galt a copy of his journal as often as convenient. Should any doubt or difficulty arise in the conduct of his mission he was to confer with such gentlemen as he thought fit, asking them to give him their opinions in writing, and he was from time to time to forward these opinions with his remarks on them. Much in this matter was necessarily being left to his own discretion but he was to bear in mind continually that whenever he incurred any expense on account of the Company it must be done with a reasonable view to a future profit equivalent to the risk incurred.[19]

The Mr. Dickson mentioned in these instructions to Dunlop was the Honourable William Dickson who was a member of the Legislative Council of Upper Canada. A native of Dumfries in the south of Scotland, he emigrated to Upper Canada in 1792, qualified for the bar, and established a law practice in the town of Niagara, then the seat of the provincial government. One of the leading patriots in the war of 1812 in which he served as an officer of Militia, Dickson dared "to treat with obvious scorn the blatant assurances of the enemy" that they came, not to conquer the Canadians, but to deliver them from oppression. He was taken in chains to Albany where he was imprisoned for two months. His house at Niagara which contained a valuable library was burned down by the enemy.

On his return to civilian life Dickson purchased from Thomas Clark a part of the Nichol block, and called it, after his birthplace, Dumfries township. With the help of Absolom Shade, a young Pennsylvania-Dutch carpenter, he established a village in the township, which the early inhabitants would have preferred to call Shade's Mills. Dickson, however, named it Galt in honour of John Galt. He and Galt had long been acquainted probably before Galt had any direct connection with Canada. Galt's first cousin, William Gilkison was Dickson's brother-in-law.

Though Galt did not say where he would be during his absence in his instructions to Dunlop, his destination was New York from which, on April 7, 1827 he sent word to the Directors that he would be in New York for about two weeks while awaiting developments. The object of his visit was to take measures with the cooperation of James A. Buchanan, the British Consul at New York, for directing the tide of emigration[20] to Upper Canada. He advised the Directors that, subject to their approval, he had, in order to secure Buchanan's services, appointed his son (whom

Galt had recommended as a suitable candidate in November 1826) as the Company's New York agent. Emigrants recommended by the new agent would be forwarded as agreed.

Galt's April letter to the Directors also mentioned that a number of families, almost all of whom had a little property, intended going to Canada and moving on to the Company's block where the town was to be laid out. He had, he added, informed these families that, should they carry out their intention, they would be granted town lots of a quarter of an acre at 20 dollars each, and that half of the money would be held in reserve to establish a fund for a school. The rate per acre quoted for town lots was, he admitted, considered low, but he felt the Directors would approve, as this principle with respect to towns and villages would reflect honour on the Company. He recommended that the 1,000,000 acre tract be laid out in as many townships as there were Directors of the Company, and named for those mentioned in the charter, and that the town to be laid out on the Company's block should be called Guelph, after the Royal family, or by some other name not yet in use. In their reply of May 11 the Directors approved of this scheme but, as regards the Grand River canal project recommended earlier, were inclined to delay action because of the expenditure of capital involved. They authorized Buchanan's appointment and gave permission for the Company's agents to make arrangements for emigrants proceeding to Upper Canada, but stipulated that emigrants were to pay their own passage.

With his New York mission satisfactorily accomplished, Galt returned to York and set the machinery for the founding of Guelph in motion. On April 22, 1827, he went, as pre-arranged, to Galt which was the nearest settlement to the Canada Company's block where the new town was to be built. At William Dickson's he joined forces with Prior and Dunlop who reported that woodmen were assembled and that everything was in readiness for the excursion to the site of the new town. They stayed overnight at Dickson's and on the morning of April 23, which was St. George's Day, Galt and Dunlop set out to cover the eighteen miles that lay between them and their objective, the woodmen under Prior having already gone on ahead. For the first nine miles they made reasonably good progress. After that, however, they got into difficulties. Dunlop had mislaid his compass and for a long time they wandered about aimlessly till they came on a hut inhabited by a Dutch shoemaker with whose assistance they succeeded in getting on course again. Further on, at the cabin of a squatter they were told that their men had all gone forward. It began to rain heavily, but they pushed on nevertheless and arrived toward evening, dripping wet, near the spot they were looking for, and at last found the men under Prior's orders kindling a roaring fire.

By the time they had done what they could to dry themselves and disposed of a hasty meal, it had stopped raining but the sun was beginning to set, so Galt proposed that they should go to the spot chosen for the town. This was the climactic moment and Galt had planned to surround it with a certain amount of ceremony. It was, as he said, consistent with his plan to invest the ceremony with a little mystery to make it memorable, yet to conduct it in such a way as to make it appear only accidentally impressive; so, intimating that the main body of the men were to wait behind, he walked to the brow of a nearby rising ground accompanied by Prior, two woodmen with their axes, and Dunlop who, having discarded his wet clothing, was dressed in blankets, Indian fashion. Prior pointed out a large maple tree marking the site selected for the town, whereupon, taking an axe from one of the woodmen, Galt initiated felling operations by delivering the first stroke, at which "the silence of the woods, that echoed to the sound, was as the sigh of the solemn genius of the wilderness departing forever." Dunlop and Prior took their turn at wielding the axe and the woodmen finished the work.

As the tree fell "with a crash of accumulating thunder," it seemed to Galt "as if ancient Nature were alarmed at the entrance of social man into her innocent solitudes with his sorrows, his follies, and his crimes"; there was a "funereal pause," a feeling in those present of the solemnity of the occasion. Dunlop, who somehow always managed to have about his person the means which he considered most appropriate when any occasion arose that seemed to call for solemnity, produced a flask of whiskey, and they all drank prosperity to the future city of Guelph. It began to rain again so they went back to the shelter of a shanty which the woodmen had put up.[21].

Some additional details with regard to the events that marked the founding of Guelph occur in a report prepared by Prior on October 1, 1827. Galt is given credit for cutting down the maple tree, which, Prior noted, stood on a "gentle eminence" about a hundred yards from the river, whence the town [when it took shape] diverged, like a fan, east, west and south. The river, a branch of the Grand, was named the Speed by Galt. On the day following the founding ceremony Galt gave orders for a start to be made on opening up a waggon road to Waterloo nine miles distant, to bring in provisions and lumber; for the building of a caravanserai; and for the clearing of the ground.[22]

The idea of the fan-like arrangement, on which the streets of Guelph were laid out, is attributed to Prior who when the maple tree was felled, is

85

supposed to have laid his hand, palm downward, with the fingers spread out fanwise on the flat top of the stump. The latter, converted into a sundial, served as the first town clock, and the severed trunk of the maple was used for one of the piers of the bridge which was in due time built across the Speed and over which in later days the railway ran.

Writing to the Directors on April 30, 1827 Galt reported that two of the families who indicated, when he met them during his visit to New York, that they were thinking of going to Upper Canada and moving on to the Guelph block, had unexpectedly arrived at Galt before accommodation for settlers at Guelph was ready. Until it was, they were being accommodated by William Dickson. Two mill sites and almost a dozen town lots had been spoken for the same day as the founding ceremony, but choosing them had been postponed until the plan of the town was finished, which it would be, sometime the following week. One important circumstance deserved mention with respect to the situation of the town. On either side of the river there were sites for no less than seventeen mills. Application had been made to the Bishop of the province for a church, likewise to Bishop Macdonell and to Dr. Harkness of Quebec, the head of the presbytery. Galt also reported to the Directors that the tract of land on which Guelph was situated was one of the finest he had yet seen and, despite its remoteness from settled areas, he would be able to sell land in it at seven shillings and sixpence an acre. This being the first settlement established by the Canada Company, he trusted that the Directors would not object to his going into these small details.

Further progress was reported when he wrote the Directors on May 31 from Guelph. In less than five weeks some fifty acres had been cleared, and a reception house constructed "in a style to which there never was anything comparable" in the country, and in which thirteen families could be comfortably lodged. It was almost ready for the accommodation of settlers, and up to the time of writing he had occupied a room in it for four days. A start had been made on a mill, several houses had been erected, and sixty-five lots were already engaged. Lack of nails and lumber was a drawback. Nearly a hundred men, nevertheless, were constantly employed, and what was particularly gratifying, there had not been a single instance of disease or any other annoying occurrence among either the labourers or the new settlers. The women and children, it was true, were still at Galt, yet so far the new settlement had been singularly fortunate, considering the state of health in Canada at that time of the year. There were at first no labourers and no one would contract at specific rates. Work had, therefore, been given to the settlers by the day, their labour being taken as payment for land, and it was hoped that in this way all the clearing and roadmaking would be completed. Town lots were selling at $20.00 per quarter acre. Bishop Macdonell had chosen sites for a church and seminary on a large scale and, Galt suggested to the Directors, he ought to get them free, since he was a member of the Company and had rendered important services to it in the early stages of its formation. Besides there were many Catholics in Guelph though generally speaking it might be called a Scottish settlement. The Church of Scotland and the Church of England, he also suggested, should get free sites when they asked for them.

More information of the same kind was contained in Galt's letter of June 14 to the Directors. Nails and lumber were still lacking. There were no well trained surveyors. The Bishop of Quebec was prepared to donate £100 towards the building of a church. A builder-speculator had arrived. Lots had been taken by three storekeepers who were presently occupying log dwellings but planned to have stone houses built. On the prospect of two millers coming from Chippewa a sawmill had been erected. Galt also brought some matters of a more general nature to the attention of the Directors. If the Company would empower him to proceed with promising schemes, he would encourage other people to erect mills and public works of that sort rather than make such things the Company's responsibility. By this arrangement the expense of a tavern and ten houses had been saved. Money was one of the rarest commodities, and because there was only one bank, financial dealings were difficult. The problem of getting suitable accommodation for himself had been solved by his procuring an unfurnished house at Burlington Bay at a rent of £150 a year, and this, with the outlay of an extra £100, would serve his purpose until an office was available. Something else had to be mentioned: Hundreds of people believed that in making payments to the Company they should be allowed to offer produce in lieu of cash.

This, we should note, was what the promoters of the Company had contended in 1824 when the terms of agreement were being thrashed out between them and the government. One of the points then in dispute was the granting of power to, or the right claimed by, the Company to trade. That could be taken to mean that the Canada Company was envisaged by its promoters as something similar to the Hudson's Bay and East India Companies. What it did mean was brought out in a letter that Simon McGillivray, one of the Directors of the Canada Company, addressed to the government. The relevant part of that letter reads as follows:

Without the power in regard to trading, it is quite idle to think of establishing any such Company [as the Canada Company]. Our declared and essential objects are to purchase Lands from the Crown

87

or other Parties, and to sell them to actual settlers, whom by the liberality of our terms, as to credit, and by the assistance held out to those who deserve it, we may induce to occupy and cultivate our Lands – This assistance is not to be given them in hard Dollars, but in the shape of a yoke of oxen, a Plough, a Waggon, Corn for Seed, or for Food . . . which, as they have no money to purchase from others, must be purchased by the Company's agents and sold to them . . . Then comes the question, how are these settlers to pay for the Lands and articles so purchased by them? . . . from the produce of the soil, a certain portion of which . . . they will deliver to the Company's Agents and such produce must be taken at a certain price, in payment of the debts previously owing to the Company.[23]

McGillivray's contention was, therefore, corroborated by the settlers referred to in Galt's letter of June 14 to the Directors. Six weeks later Galt proposed to the Directors the building of warehouses at Burlington Bay for the storage of produce received in lieu of cash payments to the Company. In the winter, he suggested, the warehouses might be used as dwelling houses. Two months elapsed before a reply came from the Directors. They advised him to proceed with the erection of the buildings at Burlington Bay but stated that the idea of taking produce in lieu of cash payments to the Company would need further consideration. Galt had already given it a good deal of consideration. He envisaged a barter system on exactly the same principle as described by McGillivray. The Company would undertake on consignment the sale of the produce it received. Furthermore, commissions on consignments of wheat would defray all official expenses and "a stimulus would be given to the prosperity of the province, which would soon compensate the country for all the profit that might be drawn from it in consequence of the Company's speculation."

It appears that he communicated these suggestions to the Directors, but in his April 30th and June 14th progress reports to them there was one thing he omitted. Having ascertained that the best site for the warehouses at Burlington Bay was "on the banks of a canal, which the government was excavating through a narrow neck of land, to open Burlington Bay into Lake Ontario,"[24] he applied to Maitland through his secretary Major Hillier for a grant of two to three acres in that location. The grant (three acres) was made subject to certain provisos;[25] but, with the application submitted to Hillier, Galt enclosed a private letter. In it, quite unnecessarily, he raked up old grievances, in particular, the dissatisfaction felt, as he alleged, by many connected with the Company at the opposition shown to its interests by influential persons in the province; and falsehoods concerning himself "the invention of which only served to prove the ignorance of the inventors as to the character of an individual, who from his very boyhood" had "neither been obscure nor in his sentiments equivocal."[26]

It gave Galt "unspeakable pleasure to have obtained for the Company so great a boon" as the site on the Burlington Bay peninsula, which he described as "much the most valuable spot in the whole province." One is left to conjecture what inspired him in requesting so great a favour to launch into a tirade. The latter produced no immediate reaction on Maitland's part, but six months later Galt would have reason to regret having written it.

The advancement of agriculture took a foremost place in Galt's efforts to give a stimulus to the prosperity of the province. In its issue of November 25, 1933, the *London Free Press* published an article entitled "Initial Farm Society Met First in 1827." The article recalled that on August 12, 1827 Galt instituted the first fair in the settlement of Guelph, then only four months old, and at a dinner attended by forty gentlemen, suggested the formation of an agricultural society which was duly formed, with Galt as first president. That was three years before the government of Upper Canada, in its concern for the rural economy, passed "An Act to encourage the establishment of Agricultural Societies in the Several Districts of the Province." At Burlington Bay Galt had an experimental farm which, on account of its situation on a plateau, he called The Mountain, and on which he planted a small vineyard, worked on the production of a refined brand of maple syrup, and, in view of the abundance of mulberry bushes in the woods adjoining the farm, speculated on the possibility of cultivating silk. The experiment, in which the Directors gave him no encouragement, was aimed at developing the resources of the province and introducing new commodities.[27]

As part of his program of community development at Guelph, Galt gave his earliest attention to the provision of education. In planning the town he stipulated that half of the price of the building sites should be used to endow a school, the Company in the first instance meeting construction costs, and being gradually repaid by the sale of the town lots. Like the making of roads, and the fostering of interest in the science of agriculture, education played an important part in Galt's colonizing strategy. The school at Guelph was one of the earliest facilities created as a means of attracting settlers. Galt's heart was set on getting a headmaster who was not only qualified in the ordinary branches of English education, but also proficient in French and Latin.[28]

When Galt wrote to Moir on August 1, 1827 he mentioned, not without a touch of pride, the things that had been or were about to be accomplished in the new town – the foundation laid for an academy, work commencing on a church, a Bank agency spoken of, a post-office, a newspaper, a market, a regular mail coach operating twice a week, and "a Khan after the Turkish fashion" capable of accommodating eighteen families – all that since April 23 when the site of the market place was in the centre of a wood miles from any habitation! The Khan, easily recognized as the caravanserai or receiving house for settlers referred to earlier in this chapter, came to be known as "the Priory," and is supposed to have got its name from Charles Prior who became the Canada Company's manager at Guelph. A Guelph newspaper, however, on the strength of a tradition handed down by a local family called Johnson, offered another explanation: Since the shanty put up by the woodmen on the campsite near the spot where the maple tree was cut down would not hold everyone, Galt ordered Prior to have a leanto of brushwood prepared to give shelter to some of the woodmen, among whom were two brothers, members of the Johnson family. One by one the men left their places at the campfire and retired to their sleeping-quarters. When Galt followed suit he discovered there was no room left in the shanty, so Prior invited him into the leanto with, "Welcome to the Priory." The actual Priory served a variety of purposes in addition to its role as a receiving house for incoming settlers. Part of it was used at one time as a prison. It was home to Galt's wife after she joined him in Upper Canada, and Guelph's first railway station. Galt intended to have it one day converted into a theatre.

The public works and roads at Guelph soon began to attract a greater influx of inhabitants than had been anticipated, and the town rose to an extent that far surpassed Galt's expectations. Where it was now spreading, all had been a wilderness,[29] and everything "was thriving beyond hope." Here, Galt reflected, were transactions which would be "memorable in the history of what must be a great country," with "neither open enmity, nor the covert machinations of personal malice, nor the ingenuity of sordid self-interest" being able thereafter to prevent his name "from being associated with the legends of undertakings at least as worthy of commemoration as the bloody traditions of heroic lands."[30] The "superb effects" obtained at Guelph were the result of "doing speedily and collectively works which in detail would not have been remarkable." It was these works that "brought 'to home' the wandering emigrants, gave them employment, and by the wonder of their greatness, magnified the importance of the improvements. This gigantic vision did not cost much more than the publication of a novel."[31]

The town was not so situated, Galt admitted, ever to become celebrated for foreign commerce, yet, from the point at which the Speed River flowed into the Grand, navigation was possible all the way to the Atlantic. Few inland towns in the whole world at such a distance from the sea could boast of such advantages;[32] and, Galt wrote:

The glory of Guelph was unparallelled . . . It consisted of a glade, opened through the forest, about seven miles in length, upwards of one hundred and thirty feet in width, forming an avenue, with trees on each side far exceeding in height the most stupendous in England.

The high road to the town lay along the middle of this Babylonian approach, which was cut so wide to admit the sun and air, and was intended to be fenced of the usual breadth, the price of the land contiguous to be such as to defray the expense of the clearing . . . A Yankee post-boy who once drove me to Guelph, on emerging from the dark and savage wood, looked behind in astonishment as we entered the opening, and clapping his hands with delight, exclaimed, 'What an almighty place!'[33]

During the spring of 1827 Galt had the pleasure of welcoming friends from Edinburgh on a sightseeing visit to Guelph, for by now the large scale operations in the settlement were beginning to be objects of curiosity. He rode across to Galt with his Edinburgh friends, intending only to give some orders there, then go right on to York, but on reaching William Dickson's they heard of the displacement of the Earl of Liverpool's government by the George Canning ministry (April 1827) and decided that the event deserved to be somehow commemorated. What could be more appropriate than a voyage of discovery? The Grand River never having been properly explored, Galt had a scow built and the party, embarking at Galt bridge, set off downstream with the current to give names to the most remarkable islands and headlands along its course. They called one peninsula which, when the snow melted, was an island, "Eldon's Doubt"; another "bold bluff promontory" that overlooked a turbulence in the stream they christened "Canning's Front"; and a violent rapid was hailed as "Horton's Hurries" in honour of one considered "accessory to" their "being in such wilds." While exploring in the woods they came upon a farmhouse and discovered to their surprise that it was called Abbotsford and that its occupant who came from Selkirk in the Scottish Borders bore the name of Walter Scott. They stayed overnight at the farmhouse and returned next day via Brantford to "the purlieus of civilization."[34]

The hectic pace of Galt's activities up to this point tends to make one lose sight of his family, but they are kept in view by the following allusions to them in Mrs. Galt's letters to her aunt in Glasgow, from March 1, 1827 onwards:

> Mr. Galt is to continue for a year or two in Canada; this I fear may be the means of my going there which on account of the voyage I would wish to avoid . . . The Directors have written to Mr. Galt requesting he would remain a year or two which is so indefinite an expression that it may mean six or seven or any term of years . . .[35]
>
> It is not yet determined whether the boys and I go out to America . . . Mr. Galt has only written to say that if I find he is to remain I must be looking forward to a voyage now. I know the Directors have written him to request he will remain for a year or two, but perhaps Mr. Galt may wish something more definite before he goes to such an expense as the removal of his family. I have no apprehension of not being comfortable . . . indeed if instead of having the prospect of enjoying every comfort that money can purchase I had the prospect of hardship and want it would still be equally my duty to go with my family where the Providence of God had sent them.[36]

> I have had a letter from Mr. Galt from which I learn I shall not need to cross the Atlantic this summer which is a great relief to my mind for although I made every exertion from a sense of duty to bring my mind to it I had but partially succeeded and might perhaps have failed at last . . . I have written for John and Tom to come home for their holidays . . . If money were plenty I would bring the boys west to see you but that is not the case, being behind in my remittances and being put to expense with the dear boys as they require . . . everything which of course I must provide before they return to school.[37]

> I have now the prospect of all the boys going with me [to Canada]. It is the country where they will most likely spend their days and of course it is my wish to be where they are as they are my dearest ties and Mr. Galt has I suppose resolved to make it his home. (he writes) 'I have got a tolerable house in a pleasant central situation. It is no very fine concern and but humbly furnished but I hope a better residence will be provided next year.' What Mr. Galt calls a tolerable house must be a pretty good one unless his views are changed from what they once were.[38]

The world knew nothing of the difficulties and anxieties Galt's family were left to contend with when he set out for Canada; and neither they nor he could foresee the problems and perplexities awaiting them "beyond the waste of seas."

Chapter 6

IN THE FOOTSTEPS
OF CHAMPLAIN

Galt resolved that an inspection would be necessary before determining the location of the Company's Huron Tract in the western part of Upper Canada. Dunlop was instructed to superintend the undertaking which, Galt had planned, should be carried out as follows. Dunlop was to assemble an exploring party at William Dickson's settlement and work his way overland to Lake Huron through the bush, while Galt was to proceed to the naval dockyard at Penetanguishene where a vessel would be waiting to convey him on a search for a natural habour somewhere along the Lake Huron shore between Cabot's Head in the north and the Aux Sables River in the south. If everything went according to plan, he and Dunlop were to meet at the mouth of one of the rivers flowing into the lake.[1]

Dunlop wrote from York, Upper Canada to his half-sister Helen on March 9, 1827:

> I am now preparing to make a dive into the woods, and shall not emerge, most probably, until mid-summer, unless something extraordinary occurs in the way . . . my love to all the folks. [2]

Mahlon Burwell, deputy to Thomas Ridout the Surveyor General at York, accompanied Dunlop and McDonald, another surveyor, on the "dive into the woods." The diary kept by Burwell throughout the expedition[3] has been drawn on for the following brief account of what befell them in the course of the expedition.

On May 12, 1827, Burwell went to Brantford. Letters from Galt and Dunlop were delivered to him there. He wrote to inform the Surveyor General that he had agreed with Galt to accompany Dunlop on an exploring expedition to Lake Huron, and the following evening rode over to Galt for dinner at William Dickson's. Early in the morning of May 14

93

he and Dunlop set out to overtake McDonald who had already left with the main body of the exploring party, and caught up with them at Smith's Creek, "called by direction of Mr. Galt, the Nith."[4]

On May 15, Burwell surveyed to the western boundary of Wilmot Township (where the Canada Company had acquired part of the Crown reserves to compensate for swampy land in the Huron Tract), and for eleven days thereafter, with some assistance from McDonald, was fully occupied in running the proof or exploratory line to Lake Huron. The ground to be covered was much swampier than expected. Once, in spite of all their efforts, the exploring party were quite unable to make their way through a cedar, black ash, pine and hemlock swamp. They had to camp in the centre of it without shelter from a rain which began falling during the night and continued into the next forenoon. The rain-sodden underbrush made work extremely disagreeable for the remainder of the day. One of the men went down with fever.

Several branches of the river called by the Indians the Menetesung (now known as the Maitland) were crossed on May 24 and finally on May 27 the line was completed to the shore of Lake Huron making, according to Burwell's figures, a total of sixty-four miles from the start-ing-point. Sixty-four miles in twelve days, was, notwithstanding the prob-lems that had arisen, a commendable achievement: but the worst problem was to come. Owing to the speed with which the line had been pushed through, coupled with the fact that the supply waggons had got stuck at a large swamp somewhere in the rear, the explorers, now encamped in a forest clearing overlooking the Menetesung where it flowed into the lake, were "destitute of a dinner." Realizing that they might wait in vain for the waggons to get through, Dunlop, (with the intention of going down river and across to Fort Gratiot, on the American side of the lake, for food,) went off with some Indians in the party to build an elm bark canoe. Next day, May 29, he dispatched a relief party to get provisions from a shanty built as a supply depot far back along the trail, and attempted to make the crossing to Fort Gratiot, but was prevented by the roughness of the lake. Rations by then had dwindled to a small piece of bread per man for breakfast, so before sunrise on May 30 Dunlop, taking five Indians with him to manage the canoe, tried for Fort Gratiot again. Because he did not return that day or the next, the rest of the party hope-fully assumed that he had succeeded. Burwell, left in charge at the camp above the river, sent one of the Indians into the woods to hunt for deer, but all he could get was five young foxes. The supply of game had improved, but only slightly, when, on July 5, a full week after setting out, Dunlop and his Indians turned up with what they had managed to find for replenishing the larder. In a letter, dated at Fort Gratiot June 2, 1827, Dunlop wrote to the "folks" at home: "We have had a most laborious journey of seventy-two miles through the woods, but have been rewarded by coming into the most beautiful country in Canada."[5]

There was still much surveying and exploring to be done by Dunlop's party in the Lake Huron area. Field operations in fact continued there till the second week in July. Burwell got back on July 13 to the point from which he had set out with Dunlop, and noted in his diary that it was two months that evening since they had entered the woods.

Galt's share in the undertaking as originally planned has now to be related. Two or three days before Dunlop's arrival at Lake Huron, he and the members of his party (unidentified by him in the *Autobiography*) set out from York for Penetanguishene on June 14, 1827.[6] They took the route by Yonge Street leading directly to Lake Simcoe, halted for the night at a place near what is now Newmarket and, on the following morning, went forward to Holland Landing. There they embarked and, descending the Holland River, steered a course across Lake Simcoe, with the boatmen, in the stillness of the evening, providing amusement "with those French airs which Moore has rendered so popular by his Canadian boat songs." At nightfall they landed near a house frequented by Indian traders and put up there until dawn when, as they were re-embarking, Galt observed the mist lying on the treetops afforded only sufficient visiblity to remind them that they were "in a far country." They touched at Innisfail where, Galt mentioned, he had a grant of land and where they learned that progress was being made with the clearing of the bush, and that some settlers had just arrived. The voyagers made another stop near the head of Kempenfelt Bay to rendezvous with a mounted party that had trekked through the forest with their luggage. The next stage of the journey was on foot along the road which Dunlop had helped to open up during the war of 1812, but it was so overgrown that it was barely possible to proceed in single file. Weather conditions forced them to take shelter overnight in a farmhouse about half way to Penetanguishene which was reached the following day by a pathway through the woods, and where, by order of the Admiralty, H. M. gunboat *Bee,* with Lieutenant Douglas in command, was standing by to go with Galt on Lake Huron. Galt and his party were billeted with the officers stationed at the dockyard, and spent two days there during which they were left pretty much to their own devices. On the third day they went aboard the *Bee* which got on course after some tacking back and forth in Gloucester Bay. They had not sailed far when a violent thunderstorm compelled them to land for the night on an island (not unlike Robinson Crusoe's, Galt thought) in the surrounding "houseless shores and shipless seas." Next morning, in the calm that succeeded the storm, they sailed for Cabot's Head, and, having rounded this "Good Hope" of the lakes, continued close inshore examining the coast carefully as they went for a possible natural harbour. It was afternoon of the following day when the dramatic moment came at which, to quote Galt,

> We saw afar off by our telescope, a small clearing in the forest, and on the brow of a rising ground a cottage delightfully situated. The appearance of such a sight in such a place was unexpected, and we had some debate, if it could be the location of Dr. Dunlop who had guided the land exploring party . . . nor were we left long in doubt, for on approaching the place, we met a canoe having on board a strange combination of Indians, velveteens and whiskers, and discovered within the roots of the red hair, the living features of the Doctor. About an hour after, having crossed the river's bar of eight feet, we came to a beautiful anchorage of fourteen feet of water, in an uncommonly pleasant small basin . . .
>
> Here we landed, and cheerfully spent the night in the log cottage which the Doctor had raised . . .
>
> Among other things which tended to make our success in finding a haven agreeable, was the production of a bottle of champagne, probably the first wine drunk on that remote spot, but not for that so remarkable as the cause. In the winter preceding, the Doctor and I returning late to York from Quebec, found ourselves hungry and exhausted; all the shops and taverns were closed, nevertheless, to wait till the morning in a semi-Christian land without refreshment, was impossible, so we sent out my servant to forage. After ransacking all houses admissable at such an hour, he returned, bringing with him two large frozen herrings or powans, and two bottles of champagne. The herrings were soon cooked, and one of the bottles discussed; the other was that which we drank on the coast of Lake Huron, and which, unknown to me, had been preserved for many months for this occasion.[7]

Burwell noted in his diary for July 1, 1827 that on June 29, about 2.00 p.m. Galt arrived at "the establishment" (the log cabin built by Burwell in the clearing where Dunlop's party had encamped) and that while Galt was there he

> named the place 'Goderich' after the estate of Mr. Robinson in England, whom he Says is now appointed Secretary for the Colonies, (of course one of the Ministry) and created Lord Goderich.

As previously noted, Galt's account in the *Autobiography* of the journey from York to Penetanguishene and the voyage on Lake Huron does not identify the members of his exploring party. That information is provided by the entry just referred to in Burwell's diary, which states that, on disembarking at Lake Huron from the *Bee,* Galt was accompanied by William Dickson, Jr. and John Brant, the Mohawk chief. That the son of the Honourable William Dickson accompanied Galt is not surprising in view of the former's interest and participation in Galt's colonizing activities; but why John Brant? The most likely explanation is the friendship that had existed between Brant and Galt since 1820. Not long after Galt was appointed agent for the Canada war sufferers, Brant arrived in London seeking a charter for the lands in Upper Canada which the British government had granted to his people, the Six Nations Indians, for their unswerving allegiance to the British flag in the war of 1812. Brant first of all delivered letters of reference to Galt, which had probably been provided by William Dickson or by Galt's cousin, William Gilkison, then pursued his business in connection with the charter through the usual governmental channels. Finding himself thwarted by bureaucratic obstructiveness he turned to Galt for help. When Galt saw the numerous "official roundabouts" Brant had received in his correspondence with the government, he "scribbled a proper tomahawk epistle" to the Secretary of State, with the result that the charter was granted. While Galt was in Upper Canada Brant called on him frequently and on one occasion mentioned that, when the chiefs of the Six Nations assembled in council heard of the tomahawk epistle, each of them gave "a particular solemn nod of approbation, like Jove in the Illiad."[8]

The day after Galt arrived at "the establishment" was spent exploring the river, after which he and his party taking Dunlop along with them re-embarked on the *Bee* and sailed down the lake, expecting to reach Detroit for the American Fourth of July festivities. For all their efforts they failed to arrive in time to take part in the celebrations but had an experience that made up for their disappointment. On the evening of July 5, accompanied by Lieutenant Douglas, the captain of the *Bee,* they went to the theatre at Detroit and, when they entered the theatre were shown to the best seats to the strains of "Rule Britannia" and "God Save The King," which Galt put down to the impression made by the captain's uniform. Galt was himself "particularly solaced afterwards by a number of Scottish airs," proposed by one of the players who knew of him. The following afternoon the *Bee* weighed anchor for Penetanguishene, while Galt and Dunlop returned by way of Buffalo and Niagara Falls to York. "Thus," Galt concluded, "ends the narrative of a voyage of discovery, in which no hardship was suffered, and much pleasure enjoyed."[9] All in all Galt's voyage of discovery had, indeed, been a rather pleasant affair. The "dive into the woods" by Dunlop and his companions was, however, a tremendous undertaking and at times a nightmarish experience which only men of invincible courage and endurance could have attempted far less survived. "They penetrated the huge untravelled wilderness, . . . in all directions having experienced and withstood every privation that wanderers can possibly be subject to in such places."[10] It was rumoured that they had been murdered by Indians, so that in some quarters they were given up as lost beyond hope of rescue in the bush.[11]

Today, one may stand on the bluff, on the very spot where Dunlop and his men emerged from the wilderness on that May Sunday almost a hundred and fifty years ago, a hundred and twenty feet above the river and the lake at Goderich. The area in which they established their base for further operations in connection with their mission, had long been a Chippewa camping ground, known only to fur traders and to Jesuits who made it a stopping-place on their way from Georgian Bay to Detroit, till Dunlop and Galt came on the scene. Among the former was W. F. Gooding, a British subject originally and United Empire Loyalist who in 1826, accompanied by his partner Frank Deschamp, arrived by the water route from Detroit to set up a post for trading with the Indians and some Métis, originating from the Hudson's Bay Company, who were also at that time encamped in the vicinity. The log cottage built by Burwell as part of the camp established by Dunlop's party stood near the site of Gooding's trading post, and with two log buildings added to it later served as the provincial headquarters of the Canada Company down to 1852. This was the nucleus of the present town of Goderich which was conceived by Galt and laid out, as is believed, on his unique spokes-of-a-wheel plan. It was at Galt's suggestion that the name of the river on which Goderich stands was changed from the Menesetung to the Maitland.

Galt wrote from Burlington Beach to Blackwood on November 30, 1827:

> This will serve to let you know that I am still in the land of the living – after the most active year of my whole life I have at last obtained a little leisure . . . but hitherto I have not had a day to spare from the road or the office . . .
>
> Besides many journeys I have been round Lake Huron and fixed upon the site of another town and in the course of a few days I have the foundation of a third to lay – the first I called Guelph – the second has been named Goderich and the third is at the request of a friend to be Muirdrum.

98

Three settlements in one year you will allow is pretty well, but they form only a small part of my labours. It is now determined that I am not to return but to remain as sole superintendent with a salary of sufficient respectablility – inferior only to that of the Governor – with the country I am much pleased. It opens out far finer than I had expected and my avocations suit my dispositon . . .

Goderich, compared with Guelph, was rather slow in developing. Indeed for quite some time after its founding it consisted of the Canada Company buildings, a log house belonging to Samuel Strickland (whom Galt recruited in Canada to work for the Company) and a tavern, on the bluff. On the flats about the river and the harbour, where most of the activity of the settlement was concentrated, some dwelling-houses and other buildings including sheds were erected by the Company to cater for incoming settlers. Most of the settlers in the early years were from Britain. At the end of the long and hazardous voyage over the Atlantic, they landed either at New York and went on to Buffalo or at Quebec or Montreal and proceeded to the head of Lake Ontario. From Buffalo they had to take the circuitous water route via Lake Erie, the Detroit River, Lake St. Clair, the St. Clair River and Lake Huron to Goderich; and from the head of Lake Ontario, the overland journey to Fort Erie and after that the above mentioned circuitous water route to Goderich. Overland from Buffalo or the head of Lake Ontario to Goderich was obviously the best route, but there was then no road from the lower terminus of the Huron Tract to Goderich, so Galt decided to make one.

Through the section of Crown reserves which the Canada Company had been granted in Wilmot township to make up for swamp land in the Huron Tract, Galt reckoned he could reach the boundary line between the townships of Wilmot and Waterloo and from there make connection with the road already opened up between Galt and Guelph. Under Prior's supervision operations were begun in the spring of 1828 as described by Galt in the *Autobiography:*

All the woodmen that could be assembled from the settlers were directed to be employed, an explorer of the line to go at their head, then two surveyors with compasses, after them a band of blazers, or men to mark the trees in line, – then went the woodmen with their hatchets to fell the trees and the rear was brought up by waggons with provisions and other necessaries. In this order they proceeded simultaneously cutting their way through the forest, till they reached their chosen destination on the lonely shores of Lake Huron, where they turned back to clear off the fallen timber from the opening behind.[12]

For this "'Caesarean operation,'" as he called it, "on the woods" Galt was allowed £3,000. The actual cost was nearly £5,000, but having stipulated that the workmen were to be paid, partly in money and partly in land, he was able to declare a final profit of more than £1,900. Because of the inadequacy of the funds provided for undertaking such a project, the quality of the work was, in his opinion, not as good as it might have been. From this it might be inferred that in the execution of the work there was not always the strictest observance of roadmaking regulations according to which not only were trees to be removed, but stumps not over a foot in diameter as well as hillocks were to be levelled to the ground. All stumps on the roadway were to be cut and grubbed, and the fifteen foot corduroys or crosstimbers laid on the roadway covered with six inches of earth and sown with grass seed. Even if all of these requirements were not always met, Galt considered the road through the Huron Tract as one of his most gratifying accomplishments. "Of one thing," he wrote, "I do not hesitate to say I was proud, and with good reason too: – I caused a road to be opened through the forest of the Huron Tract, nearly a hundred miles in length, by which an overland communication was established, for the first time, between the two great lakes, Huron and Ontario."[13]

Essential to the usefulness of this road (and others like it) were the inns located at twenty mile intervals along its entire length, such as McConnel's Tavern a description of which was given by William Proudfoot, a Presbyterian minister whose diary records his observations and experiences on a trip from London to Goderich in 1833. In the entry for Thursday, February 28 Proudfoot wrote:

The tavern . . . near the north side of the Township of Usborn . . . is ordered by the Canada Company . . . to accommodate travellers. It is one of the most wretched places I ever spent a night in. The logs are not well built, the interstices are very carelessly filled up, there is no clay or lime, the wind finds its way between the logs at almost every place. The door did not fit by at least three or four inches. There was kept on an enormous fire which served to produce a draft of air which was directed up the chimney by the heat and made us colder before the fire than out of doors. There were at least nine lodgers in the house. Mr. Christie and I occupied one of the beds, a very poor concern indeed. The innkeeper and his wife occupied the other. All the rest squatted . . . in a lump with their feet towards the fire and their bodies wrapped in such coverings as they had brought with them, or as the house could furnish. Though Mr. Christie and I did the best we could to keep ourselves warm, in spite of all I could do, I was forced to rise and warm myself. We were nothing the worse for our sleep in this shanty . . .[14]

The date at which the reverend gentleman was subjected to such rigours has to be taken into account. By 1833 the Canada Company had become lax in its ways and in many respects indifferent to the needs of those it professed to serve. Even before then, however, the inns along the road, like the bed occupied at McConnel's by the minister and his companion, were no very great affairs; but in addition to providing accommodation for travellers like Proudfoot or for settlers proceeding to their holdings on the Canada Company's lands, they served the important purpose of keeping the road open during the winter. For performing this service the innkeepers were paid a bounty which increased in proportion to their distance from more settled areas.

No matter, it has been said, how fine the quality of the land in the Huron Tract, "without the Huron Road, rough as it was, many settlers would have experienced much greater difficulty in reaching their chosen lots." Compared with the typical pioneer roads which "were usually built after settlement at the request or demand of the people," the Huron Road "was unique in that it was built through virgin forest to encourage settlement,"[15] and in particular to attract the kind of settler Galt was most anxious to secure. When he wrote from New York on April 7, 1827 to Horton providing statistical information relating to emigrants from the United Kingdom, Galt noted the great and increasing number of people who, having been for some time in the United States, were moving to Canada, of which he went on to say:

> The country is filled with small prosperous proprietors ambitious and uneducated and the whole system of settlement . . . is only calculated to breed democrats – The system of emigration would work infinitely better and redound more to the common good of the empire, were some principle laid down which in operation would evolve the establishment of an *aristocracy*.[16]

James Clarke Buchanan, the Company's agent at New York, had just issued a brochure announcing that speculators would not be encouraged but that every encouragement would be given to sober and industrious men with families. No one, it was stated, would be admitted into any society of location, for a town or village, who could not produce satisfactory testimonials of good character, as no society could prosper where religion, morality and industry were not united.[17]

Goderich "was fortunate in its first settlers, folk of British stock, poor in this world's goods but rich in industry and courage," who "left their imprint in family and place names – English in Goderich Township, . . . Irish in the Tipperary section, Scottish about Smith's Hill."[18] Early or late the Scots made their presence felt. There were times when "the air was . . . full of 'the clash of broadswords and the din of gathering clans,' " the Scots not being "dazzled by any species of elevation, and" carrying "their burr into whatever haunts ability" might "take them . . . these were all 'great fechters. They fought as they prayed, and they prayed as they fought,' "[19] with "Tiger" Dunlop ever ready to lead them in the fray.

Typical of the aristocratic element Galt considered so desirable was a Mr. Cook[20] who had "a number of paintings representing the pleasures of the chase" which "had once figured on the walls of some house in Prince's (sic) Street, Edinburgh," hanging in his rustic home near Goderich; and Daniel Lizars whose interest in the adventures of British colonial pioneers, a topic much discussed by his family, may have been quickened into action by a notice of the following sort appearing in some British newspaper:

Canada Company. To Emigrants arriving from the United Kingdom:

Along the road from Wilmot to Goderich, the land, which is all of the best quality, will be sold in lots of 100 acres, each, for which at the option of the purchasers, payment at the rate of 7s.6d. per acre, will be taken in cash, provisions, or labour on the roads from the first two hundred heads of families who offer themselves as settlers and supplies of provisions and medical assistance will be provided by the Company. Saw and grist mills are building near the proposed site of Goderich . . .

May 28. 1828. John Galt, Superintendent.

Lizars, whom Proudfoot met in his travels, and described as "brother to the bookseller, the engraver and doctor of the same name" and as "a land surveyor and draftsman,"[21] had embarked for New York on the *Science,* with all his worldly goods, his widowed mother, his wife, and seven children. From New York he proceeded by canal and lake boat to Detroit, where he chartered the *Rob Roy* and made for Goderich. A violent storm blew up half way, and Macgregor the owner and captain of the ship was suddenly stricken with a severe attack of ague. Lizars had to take command. He managed somehow to navigate the *Rob Roy* through the darkness and the storm, and, sighting Goderich early on a Sunday morning, ran her aground on the harbour bar. Settlers of his type were rich not only in industry and courage, but also in the finer things of life. Surviving the hazards of the journey to Goderich was a small rosewood upright piano which he brought all the way from Edinburgh.[22]

In a long letter to his sister, dated August 1, 1827 at Burlington Beach[23] Galt wrote:

> I have no society such as I have been accustomed to, and having a great deal of personal fatigue, I have felt at times more weary than the exertion alone would have caused. It has pleased God however to give me extreme good health. I have never felt myself so well. But still being so much alone, so often solitary in the woods and so frequently a sojourner in . . . inns, I greatly feel this want of my family.

The sense of loneliness he experienced is brought vividly home by his reference in the *Autobiography* to his habit of wandering alone in the summer evenings in the forest.[24] He had no books, he said, "to withdraw" his "mind" from things that worried and upset him.[25] All that, however, would soon be changed when his wife and family joined him. In his letter of August 1 he told his sister:

> I have written to her to come out with Alec in the fall and in the spring I intend to bring John, and Tom. It would seem that my home is to be in this Country, and my business is more congenial to my disposition and turn of mind than anything I ever was engaged in. I hope it will prove successful and that I shall be able to conduct it with satisfaction to the Company and the settlers.

In only a few years the success he hoped for was beginning to be realized in the vastly improved conditions in the Huron Tract and the surrounding area, though he was not there to see them. Samuel Strickland recalled that on his visit to the mouth of the Maitland River in 1829, a seventy mile bridle-path through the trackless forest was the only available communication between Guelph and Lake Huron. That vast and fertile tract of more than one million acres did not contain a population of 300 souls; no teeming fields of golden grain, no manufactories, no mills, no roads; the rivers were unbridged, and one vast solitude reigned around. In no great time the scene had been remarkably transformed. Stage coaches travelled with safety and despatch along the same track where formerly the traveller had had the utmost difficulty in making his way on horseback without being swept from the saddle by the limbs of trees and tangled brushwood. A continuous settlement of the finest farms skirted both sides of the road from the southern boundary of the district to Goderich.[26] The following extract from a statistical account of Goderich and district showed how conditions had changed by 1841:

> This splendid district, consisting of a million acres, is bounded by the Wellington, London and Western District, extends a long distance on the shores of Lake Huron, and will be united with the new settlement opening by the Government, extending from Garrafranca to Owen Sound ... Perhaps no portion of Canada presents a finer appearance, is cultivated better or is in a more thriving state. The [Canada] Company have opened a wide road to Goderich on Lake Huron. It ... unites 12 miles from Goderich with the other main road which has been made by the Company through their land from the Township of London ... Near the Village of Stratford upon Avon are several beautiful lakes on the road side ... The Company have an office also here for public information ... From the centre of the township of Fullarton and throughout the township of Hullet, the aspect of the country greatly improves. There are larger quantities of land in cultivation, more houses, greater abundance of stock, and more agricultural produce is raised.
>
> On reaching the township of Goderich the prospects appear still more gratifying, the settlements on the road side being continuous and prosperous, and the first habitations generally giving way to better dwelling houses ...
>
> Nothing can exceed the beauty of the situation of the Town of Goderich. It is high dry and extremely salubrious. One portion is situated nearly on the level of the River Maitland and the other on the high and lofty tableland forming its bank commanding a most extensive view of the lake and the Maitland River which divides Goderich from Colborne and which runs from the interior of the country through high hills skirted at their base by a rich valley ... as the settlement of township[s] bordering on the lake progresses, the trade and prosperity of Goderich must also proportionably advance, as there is no other port on that shore of Lake Huron where vessels can take refuge in storms.

We can form a more general idea of the changes brought about by Galt's work as colonizer in Upper Canada in the light of certain observations made by John Howison during the two and a half years that he spent in the province collecting material for the information of immigrants, which appeared in book form in 1821. One of Howison's first impressions was the poor state of agriculture in already settled areas, the Thames district in particular, of which he wrote as follows:

> Both sides of the river have been settled, and under cultivation, during more than thirty years; however, the uninquiring traveller would suppose that they had but recently known the presence of man . . . miserable log-huts, ill-ploughed fields, shackling barns, and unpruned orchards, are to be seen every where, disfiguring the face of the country, and shewing too accurately the character of those who inhabit it. This settlement, I was informed, had undergone little change or advance within the last ten years, and, consequently, it has reached the highest pitch of improvement it will probably ever attain while in the hands of its present occupants.[27] . . . There is hardly a clean or a well-ploughed field in the western part of the Province; nor has any single acre there, I believe, ever yielded nearly as much produce as it might be made to do under proper management[28] . . . for the Canadians have as yet paid very little attention to any of the branches of horticultural science[29] . . . The Canadian farmers have no system in their agricultural operations, or in the management of their lands . . . These circumstances are generally the result of ignorance, but often arise from a want of capital.[30]

Other impressions made on Howison were: the lack of proper education and religious facilities, the relatively uncivilized character of people long established in some of the older settled areas, and the bad state of the roads. He also found himself "occupied with reflections upon the helpless condition of most of the emigrants who came to Canada," and the indifference of the government with regard to the welfare and the prosperity of the colony. People, he noted, who came to the province as intending settlers had no means whatever of obtaining reliable information about where they were meant to go or about where or how they should apply for a grant of land. They could not be, he commented, expected to struggle resolutely with the difficulties that faced them on every side, "ignorant of the country," as they were, "and often disappointed with it at *first*," the "slaves of vague reports, and false and exaggerated descriptions" of what awaited them, and "after being alternately encouraged, depressed, and deceived . . . perhaps prematurely" determined "to return to their native country," however wretched the asylum it might afford.

The majority of such people, Howison reported, had enough money to pay their way to, and get comfortably settled in, the upper province, but when they landed they were detained in Lower Canada "by anxious and unavailing efforts to obtain correct information" regarding the "promised land." All this could have easily been prevented, and thousands of settlers added annually to the province if the government had given it a moment's thought, and located at Quebec, Montreal, and other places agents to whom emigrants could apply for assistance and advice.[31]

It was not at first glance an encouraging or very prepossessing picture. Nevertheless, Howison, on the overall view, could write hopefully, indeed prophetically:

> He who takes a general survey of Upper Canada will . . . find abundant room for interesting speculation, whether he considers the physical improvements of which the country is eminently susceptible, or anticipates the grandeur and importance it must eventually attain; but it would be vain and useless to indulge in views of this kind, until the prosperity of the Province is established upon more sure foundations than it is at present, and an increase of wealth and population secures to it the means of carrying into effect those plans and arrangements that would elicit its capabilities.[32]

All the deficiencies Howison lamented, Galt made provision for with the machinery he devised and set in motion when he established his model settlements at Guelph and Goderich. As MacTaggart wrote in his *Three Years in Canada:*

> The [Canada] Company . . . are ready at all times to give every information and assistance, so as to enable emigrants to get out in the quickest and most economical manner possible . . . agents at the different seaports of the United Kingdom have been . . . furnished with maps of Upper Canada, and diagrams of every township in which any of the lands assigned to the Company are situated, to be shown to all persons intending to go out; . . . The agents at Montreal and New York (the two principal routes to Upper Canada) will give them every information and assistance; . . . The object of the Company is . . . to open access to the settlement of the lands by a steady and industrious agricultural population . . . To settlers who are well recommended, and who may in the beginning require assistance in commencing the cultivation of their farms, or providing for their families, until they can raise a crop from their own lands, the Company's Superintendent is authorized to advance, on security, the needful supplies at his discretion, but only to such as may be considered to merit the same.

In using his discretion in such matters Galt was sometimes prone to err – on the side of humanity. He would not drive squatters off the Company's

106

lands, but sold them the land on which they had squatted, to their advantage and that of the Company, "considering the little *clearings* they had made, as *uncleared* forest. By doing this he ... established a class of people in the townships devoted to the interest of the Company."[33] He was "a true friend of the early settlers ... was on their ground, knew their problems, and cherished a far vision of what this land must ultimately be. If a settler was unable to pay his instalment, what of it? The man was honest and the land was good."[34]

Chapter 7

A RAVELLED SKEIN OF CARE

The heading of this chapter which is borrowed from Galt's *Autobiography*[1] well describes the mounting toll of perplexities and troubles in which from now on he began to find himself.

There was first of all the La Guayra emigrants affair which arose at the time when, considering it more convenient for the conduct of business to have his headquarters located half way between York and Guelph, Galt took up residence on the Burlington Beach peninsula. He had not been long settled there when, as he wrote in the *Autobiography:*

> One Sunday morning a deputation came to me, from a body I think, in all, of fifty-seven emigrants, who had come from New York, where they had been landed from La Guayra in South America. They were part of the settlers whom the Colombian Company had enticed to transport themselves to that region, where being disappointed and reduced to great necessity, they were for a time obliged to subsist on charity . . .[2]

"By October 19th, 1826, the failure of the colony was apparent." The Colombian Agricultural Association or, as Galt calls it, the Colombian Company "was touching on bankruptcy, allowances and rations to the settlers had ceased and they were beginning to abandon their few acres."[3] Not long afterwards the settlers almost all of whom were Scots petitioned both houses of Parliament, and the British government authorized the granting to them of relief and repatriation allowed to British subjects discharged from mining or other associations for misconduct and other causes.

Although the British government had authorized repatriation, the majority of the settlers were attracted to Canada. This was probably because Alexander Cockburn, recently appointed the first British Minister at Bogota, the capital of Greater Colombia, had given them the impression that they would receive free provisions and grants of land if they went to Canada, and because Cockburn's younger brother Francis, who, it will be recalled, was chairman of the commission appointed to assess the value of the lands offered for sale to the Canada Company, was already in Canada arranging for the settlement of poor emigrants.

The idea appears to have been that those among the La Guayra settlers who wished to go to Canada should occupy part of the Crown lands in Upper and Lower Canada and in Nova Scotia. Passages were provided for them at the expense of the British government, and on June 18, 1827, the exodus began. A first contingent on arrival at New York were committed, notwithstanding the presence of the British consul there, as Ker Porter the British consul in Venezuela had directed, to the care of Charles Moore who represented shipping interests. When a second contingent arrived they were placed in the custody of the British consulate where it was felt that Moore had been brought in by mistake; but the consul, James A. Buchanan, was absent at the time, so his elder son, James Clarke Buchanan who was British vice-consul and also agent for the Canada Company at New York, took charge of the settlers. After some deliberation he decided to have them sent to the Canada Company's agent at Niagara for transmission to Upper Canada. Buchanan assumed, as he explained in a letter to Galt, that the agent at Niagara would have instructions regarding the settlers, and that Francis Cockburn would still be at York where he had been on July 10, 1827 for consultation with Sir Peregrine Maitland. Cockburn had, however, shortly after July 10 gone to Quebec en route for England.

On July 17, 1827 the settlers left New York and reached Burlington Bay on the 30th. They had letters from the Minister and the consul in Colombia to show that they were being sent at the expense of the British government, in the expectation that an emigration department had been set up at Halifax, Nova Scotia. No such arrangement had been or was being made by the time the settlers turned up at Burlington Beach, so Galt arranged that they should be provided for at Guelph until a decision was reached as to what should be done with them. These unfortunate victims of bureaucratic mismanagement were in a wretched state. Ague and malaria were rife among them, particularly among the women and children, thirty-seven of the latter being under fourteen years of age. Having no resources for the support of unproductive and pauper settlers, Galt withheld £1,000 from a £20,000 payment then due to the provincial government by the Canada Company. He was convinced that the Colonial

Office would see the absolute necessity of the measures he had adopted and that a settlement could be made between the British government and the Company, unless Maitland saw fit to relieve him of the consequences of the unforeseen emergency that had arisen.

He reported what had happened to Horton, to the London headquarters of the Company, and to Maitland whose views he requested on the disposal of the settlers. Maitland did not reply. Galt then went to York to interview the Receiver General and, to spare him any inconvenience and at the same time to let Maitland see in what spirit he had acted, said that he would hand over the £1,000 he had withheld on the understanding that it was "in doubt for the Guayrians" till the problem created by their arrival was cleared up. By August 21 there was still no response from Maitland so Galt reported to Horton that he had decided to do something about solving the problem himself. Gathering the Guayrians together he offered them the opportunity of settling on the Canada Company's lands and explained the terms of settlement: Each family would be granted fifty acres, at ten shillings an acre, to be supplemented, once they were established on their holdings, by another fifty acres at that price. Because of their destitution they would not be required to make an initial payment, but would be expected to discharge their debt plus interest at 6 per cent per annum over a stated period. Further, to enable them to earn some income, all the able-bodied men would be employed at the common rate in making roads. The offer was accepted by the Guayrians, and a start was made on erecting houses for them, which they would be left to finish themselves, while the children were sent to school.

More settlers from La Guayra arrived. On September 22 Galt reported to Horton that the newcomers were in good health and that they would be provided for in the same way as those preceding them who, with their ailments behind them, their houses going up, and their lands on the way to being cleared, were already paying their way with the help of loans from the Company.

There was some disquiet at the Foreign Office and the Colonial Office about procedural irregularities brought to light in communications received by them from Ker Porter and from Galt. The Colonial Office first heard of the predicament of the settlers in Venezuela when Ker Porter drew on the treasury for £100 to meet the cost of supporting them. The Treasury's main concern, as its correspondence with Horton apprising him of the problem indicated, was to get the settlers out of Venezuela. The move seems to have proceeded on the assumption that the Colombian Agricultural Association had guaranteed to defray whatever expenses were incurred on the settlers' behalf. The Colonial Office, considering that they might be held financially responsible for the settlers now located in Upper Canada and surmising from Galt's letters that he might also be running them into expense, protested strongly to the Foreign Office and to the Directors of the Canada Company. The Foreign Office and the Colonial Office, it transpired, acted in ignorance of all the circumstances and exaggerated the extent to which the Government was committed by the supposed irregularities. It would, therefore, not be too much to say that Galt was made the scapegoat for the censurable behaviour of Alexander Cockburn and Ker Porter on the one hand, and for the ill-informed handling of the situation by the government on the other.

The Directors of the Canada Company apologized to the Colonial Office for Galt's excess of zeal, gave assurance that he would do as he was told by the provincial authorities, and appealed to that office "to take a humanitarian view of the plight of these distressed British subjects thrown helpless into the Canadian woods with winter coming on." At the same time they admonished Galt for taking things into his own hands, for withholding the £1,000 and for causing considerable embarrassment both by failing to act in consultation with the provincial government and by undermining the guarantee of the Colombian Agricultural Association. They advised him to proceed with the disposal of the emigrants in accordance with the wishes of the provincial government and to hand over the £1,000 immediately.

Galt could not let that pass unnoticed. He wrote to Horton rebutting the charge of bypassing the provincial government. The plight of the emigrants, he protested, had required immediate attention and he had not decided to do anything about it until there seemed to be no likelihood of a response to his request for instructions from the government at York. He had not been aware of any guarantee on the part of the Colombian Agricultural Association or of the fact that Buchanan was acting in his capacity as vice-consul. The £1,000 had not been needed after all and the emigrant fares from New York to Guelph, which had been paid for by the consul at New York, was the sum total of expenses that the government had incurred. He also wrote on December 24, 1827 to the government expressing the hope that the provincial authorities would make clear to the Colonial Office that his action regarding the settlers had been dictated by the urgency of the matter. What was he supposed to do with them? Turn them adrift in the woods?

Meantime there had been murmurs of discontent from the settlers. They felt they had been deceived about the prospect of free land grants in Upper Canada and that they were now being imposed on by the Company in that they were required to finish by themselves the houses erected for them, whereby their indebtedness to the Company had been increased by £20 to £30. On December 26 Galt demanded that an enquiry be set up by the provincial government to look into these complaints. Maitland's reply took the form first of a complaint. He would, he told Galt, no longer receive any communications from him couched in such offensive terms, but promised that the Executive Council would take the matter in hand. On January 29, 1828, Maitland was handed the results of the enquiry. He was, it announced, exonerated from charges of failure to act, since he had properly assumed that the Canada Company had taken complete charge of the emigrants at the time of their arrival; no intervention had then been called for on his part; only some time after that had it become apparent that the settlers had been sent from New York to Canada by the vice-consul, and not by the Canada Company's agent.

In the report Galt was singled out for blame. It was alleged that he had bypassed the provincial government as demonstrated by the casual way in which he had sent to his superiors the letters of recommendation from Cockburn and the consul at Caracas, that, as a private individual and as representative of a private company, he had usurped the functions of government, had interfered in arrangements made between the latter and the Colombian Agricultural Association,[4] and withheld money due to the government. The settlers, it was asserted, had been sent by officials to the charge of officials in Canada, though they expressed their satisfaction with the manner in which the Canada Company was treating them and the way things were working out for them, despite their disappointment at not receiving free grants of land.

Against the assertion that no intervention had been called for on Maitland's part has to be set the fact that on November 7, 1827 he had been authorized by the Secretary of State to afford the settlers such indispensable relief as he might deem expedient till he should receive further instructions on how to dispose of them. The Secretary of State, however, let it be distinctly understood that he was to disavow any claim Galt might feel disposed to make for any expenses previously incurred on the settlers' behalf. After the enquiry Maitland wrote to the Colonial Office saying that in view of the recommendations handed down as a result of the enquiry, he preferred not to interfere with the settlers from South America, since they were already under contract to the Canada Company, and Galt was in agreement. At the same time Maitland wrote to the Secretary of State complaining of the peremptory tone of Galt's representations to the provincial government on behalf of the settlers, and stating that although such behaviour would not be prejudicial to the Company, he had to acknowledge candidly that so far as he was concerned, it could by no means be regarded as calculated to establish "a more unreserved intercourse" between Galt and the provincial authorities.

Galt was given no credit for the satisfactory outcome of the muddle over the La Guayrians, to the clearing up of which the provincial government had made no positive contribution. He was not even reimbursed for the money which, as he mentioned in a note to the government, he paid out of his own pocket for the relief of the La Guayrians. As for the latter, they continued to work, for, and earn their livelihood with, the Canada Company till Galt ceased to be superintendent. Not long after that they were scattered throughout the adjoining townships to begin the battle of life all over again in the deeper recesses of the bush,[5] having by that time fully discharged their indebtedness to the Company.

It was beginning to be rumoured that Galt's expenditures at Guelph were tending to lower the value of the Company's stock; and, to add to his discomfort, the Directors started squabbling with him over the naming of the settlement. In conveying his apologies for this to the Directors on September 29, 1827 he explained that by the time that political changes in England became known in Canada the place had really become of public interest. He asked for a list of names which would be considered suitable, pointing out that, drawing on their reminiscences, the settlers often gave names to places themselves. Some twenty persons, he reported, had sent in an application to have a village laid out for them in the Company's block in Vaughan, and, if it were found advisable to accede to the proposal, the place would be called Muirdrum.

The Directors' response reached him on November 29. They drew his attention to the fact that "Goderich" had been suggested as the name of the first settlement as a compliment to His Majesty's Chief Secretary of State, and accordingly that name had been used in the Company's prospectus. They also stated that the royal name should be given to some extensive district such as the one million acres tract. Because the name already given to the settlement could not be changed except by an Act of the provincial government it was adopted by the Court, and the Court promised an explanation to the Secretary of State. Approval was also given for laying out the proposed village in Vaughan. The Court had no objection to settlers naming villages or settlements, but townships, counties and other territorial divisions were generally named by authority of the government.

The report drawn up by Prior on October 1, 1827 on the operations at Guelph was submitted to the Directors, but they did not consider it satisfactory. They pointed out to Galt that money had been used extravagantly without being adequately accounted for. The Court, he was told, was "most anxious on the subject of unchecked expenditure."

A warning Galt received from Horton to be more circumspect towards the officers of the government[6] does not seem to have perturbed him overmuch. He found more cause for concern in a private letter sent to him by one of the Directors in late December to inform him that a complaint made against him by Maitland had been passed through Stanley, Horton's successor as under-secretary at the Colonial Office, to Colonial Secretary Huskisson who had communicated it to the Directors, and that he was to be reprimanded by the latter for insulting the Lieutenant-Governor. Galt called on Maitland to discover what this was about. Maitland denied that he had at any time complained of Galt's insulting him but admitted that he had been in communication with London regarding the letter Galt had written to Hillier on applying for the land at Burlington Bay.

In their dispatches of November 5, 1827, to Galt, enclosing copies of the letters that had passed between him and Hillier and Maitland, the Directors spoke of the displeasure felt by the Secretary of State at what was alleged to have transpired and voiced their disapproval of the tone pervading Galt's side of the correspondence, particularly some of the remarks that he had made. They were, they said, in general agreement with the government and would not be associated with his grievance because it had provoked opposition to the Company; they rebuked him for the vague and mysterious nature of his complaints, not to mention his idea that certain "influential persons" were working against the Company's interests; and expressed their satisfaction as to the friendly attitude of the Lieutenant-Governor. Being unaware of any misrepresentations injurious to Galt personally, and therefore unable to judge of them, they considered that explanation would not improve matters and advised him to forget what had happened if possible; yet they could not conclude without expressing their undiminished confidence in his zeal and his best exertions on behalf of the Company and acquitted him of any intention to give offence to the provincial government. They had, nevertheless, to communicate to him their desire that in all future application to and correspondence with the provincial government he would carefully avoid the introduction of any allusions to supposed opinions or feelings either of any member of that government or of the Court of Directors. This concurred with the wish expressed by the Lieutenant-Governor that all forthcoming communications with him on the business of the Company should be strictly official. The Directors felt that in all future dealings Galt should try for the good of all to forget entirely what was past. The Court was ready to support him in every possible way, but had to be satisfied of the strict justice and propriety of their claims on his behalf. There had for some months, they stated, been no replies to letters submitted to the government, and no access to it for the Company, which had caused a good deal of impatience. Now, to the great regret of the Court it was ascertained that much of the difficulty had arisen from the impressions produced by the tenor of Galt's correspondence with the provincial authorities; and whether, which was doubted, in the tone and substance of his letters, he had expressed the Court's sentiments or his own.

The Directors were convinced that without the countenance and favour of the government, the Company could not prosper and ought not to go on. It was therefore essential to the prosperity of the Company that its superintendent or representative should not be prominent as a political opponent or as the intimate associate or supposed instrument of the political opponents of the provincial government. It was evident that Galt had been considered to stand in that light, whether justly or unjustly the Court did not decide; but so far as they could judge from newspaper paragraphs and reports of speeches, it certainly did appear that he had given ground for that supposition. The Court had resolved to state the case frankly to him in the hope that such collision of his opinions with those of the government or of the Clergy Corporation might not appear in the same public manner thereafter. The Directors also took exception to his advertizing sites for churches or other places of public worship, and burying grounds for congregations of any religious denominations which, by a resolution of the Court passed on July 6, 1827, he had been authorized to provide. That resolution, they pointed out, was meant for his own guidance but not for publication as an advertisement, and its appearance as such in the *Colonial Advocate* was regretted. Besides, it was probable that the frequent appearance of the Company's armorial bearings and the praise of the Company's superintendent and his proceedings as contrasted with other parties in that particular paper, would in reality rather be injurious than advantageous to the Company's interests, since the source of that praise or the motive to which it might be ascribed could not be very satisfactory to the provincial government.

The Directors regretted having to say all this. Mr. Secretary Huskisson's letter, however, left them no choice and imposed on them the necessity of taking a decided ground on this communication with the government both in England and in Canada. If there were parties in Upper Canada the Company must be of the government party and its representatives must abstain from any course offensive to the authorities without whose countenance and cooperation its proceedings must at every step be impeded and its success rendered hopeless.

Regret was expressed by the Directors for what had given rise to their communications. The Court had an extremely painful duty to perform. Their discharge of it was dictated solely by their conviction of its essential importance to the interests of the Company, and they could not in deference to their strong feeling of individual regard for Galt's personal comfort shrink from maintaining these interests.

Galt was offended by the Directors having jumped to the conclusion that he was guilty before giving him an opportunity to speak up for himself. He felt that he had been done a great injustice and that the construction put on his letter by Hillier was unwarranted and erroneous. Though he had communicated his correspondence with Maitland to Horton, he had not at first considered the matter worth drawing to the attention of Bosanquet, the chairman of the Directors. He now sent in his resignation but it was not accepted.

While this wrangle was going on preparations were in progress for the long remembered Canada Company ball with which, on New Year's Eve, 1827 Galt planned to bedazzle and delight the inhabitants of York. It took place, we are told,

> At Francks', one of the inns whose comfort is so criticized in the 'Autobiography.' Like all places of the kind, it had its large assembly room. The decorations were elaborations of the Company's Arms; . . . 'The sides and ceiling of the room and passages leading to it were made bowers of green with hemlock and spruce, lit with innumerable coloured lamps bearing floating lights.'[7]

When Galt staged this extravaganza, he was under the impression that there had lately been a "gradual softening in many things" towards him. Colonel Coffin, the head of the militia department, had mentioned to him quite recently that Maitland was considering appointing him to the command of a regiment, and that he might give some thought to which of the Company's employees would make suitable officers.[8] Perhaps one may conclude from this gesture on Maitland's part that he had not taken so much to heart as the Canada Company Directors the letter Galt sent to Hillier. The ball was, socially speaking, a splendid occasion. It also provided Galt with a good opportunity to capitalize on the "gradual softening" towards him. Unfortunately, it produced the exact opposite effect. In September, 1827 John Walpole Willis on his appointment as a puisne judge (a Superior Court judge of lower rank than chief justice) had arrived with his mother, his sister, and his wife, Lady Mary Willis, daughter of the Earl of Strathmore, to take up residence at York. Galt had to choose someone to act as hostess at the ball. Protocol would have suggested Lady Sarah Maitland, the wife of the Lieutenant-Governor. Galt's choice, however, was Willis's wife.

Some time after the New Year's Eve festivities Galt happened to meet Colonel Coffin in the street and asked him what had become of the militia appointment. Coffin appeared not to know for certain. All he could say was that Maitland had desired him to keep it back;[9] but the cause was not far to seek. By passing over Lady Sarah Maitland in his choice of a hostess for the ball Galt had committed in her eyes and in Maitland's an almost unforgiveable sin. Although Galt pretended to make light of the withholding of the militia appointment, a significant comment on how much it really meant to him was that when he sat toward the end of his life for the portrait presented to him by the James Watt Club of Greenock, he asked to be portrayed in the uniform of a colonel of the Upper Canada militia.

John Thomson, the clerk in the Company's office at York, reported to the Directors on February 11, 1828 that Galt had got badly bruised and injured internally by falling from his horse in the forest while on the way to Cornwall, and since then had been quite ill. Thomson also reported that Galt was suffering from opthalmia attended with considerable fever but that the doctor was hopeful that the sight of both eyes would be restored. About this time Galt got word that his wife and family would soon be on their way to Canada. He had completely recovered from his illness by mid-March when they were due to arrive, and went down to New York to meet them. The family now happily re-united proceeded to the house at Burlington Bay.[10]

On April 3, 1828, Galt heard from the Directors that they intended sending out Thomas Smith to work with him in the capacity of cashier and accountant, and on May 21 was advised by them that Smith was on the eve of departure from London to take up his appointment. Galt in a prompt reply from York on May 27 expressed his pleasure at the prospect of having an official coadjutor, which would relieve his attention to many details, and although it could not increase his zeal for the Company, would afford him time to furnish more explicit information to the Court and endeavour to make his service more effectual. All he had to ask, which he was sure there was no wish to deny, was a candid interpretation of his actions, and that in personal matters he might not be required to trouble the Directors. His interest and inclinations, he said, were as much interwoven with the prosperity of the Company as theirs; a sense of obligation and of individual friendship bound him to the members of the Court.

Things, however, were not as promising as they appeared to be. Galt went on a business trip to Montreal where he learned from fairly reliable sources that the general opinion in London business circles was that the Canada Company could not go on, and that its stock was falling in value; it was in fact soon selling at a discount. For Galt, the effects of the Company in promoting the prosperity of the province were of primary importance and, provided they continued, he did not care who the shareholders were. He went on with his plans for the benefit, as he thought, of the Company and the advantage of the province by opening roads to render remote lands accessible as well as more valuable and by giving employment to poor emigrants, in the belief that to these two objects everything else was subordinate.[11] However, he "could not think without wincing at the idea of being father to a wild and ruinous scheme."[12]

He returned home in July to discover that Smith had arrived from England. At first he felt gratified about this because up till then he had had to make do with fewer clerks than were necessary; but when he looked over Smith's instructions from the Directors it appeared to him that they were strangely framed, and it struck him as odd, in view of the complaints of the Directors about his own apparent extravagance, that Smith's salary seemed to be much in excess of the duties required of him. The only conclusion Galt could come to was that this was a bait to get Smith out of the way and enable him to cope with the exigencies of his situation when the time came to break up the Company.[13]

Something else that transpired during Galt's trip to Montreal suggests that he had come to the conclusion that the Company was doomed, and that he had better begin looking out for himself. On June 22, 1828 he wrote to the Earl of Dalhousie submitting the draft of a plan he had devised for the founding of a new colony, to be called Hibernia, in the northeastern region of Lower Canada. With only the Canada Company's establishment as it then existed at Guelph, he told Dalhousie, the plan could be carried into effect as soon as a portion of the country could be surveyed; and, in his estimate of the total cost involved, he put his salary at £2,000 per annum. Dalhousie, however, did not think the project feasible. Nevertheless, on his return from Montreal, Galt wrote Dalhousie again on August 13 from Guelph regarding the plan he had submitted to him on June 22, but was still unable to gain his approval for it or otherwise enlist his active interest.[14]

Toward the middle of September he wrote to the Directors saying that it grieved him that he had been thought extravagant and that it had not been his good fortune to please them when that was what he had consistently striven to do. Some days later Smith reported to McGillivray in London that he had been busy at Guelph and had found his task more difficult than he expected it would be; that Galt had made some good arrangements in the anticipation that they would be carried out, but that the men in the office had done no more than they chose to. Smith went on to say that he was worried and hampered by lack of funds; that the workmen were clamouring for pay which was due to them and that in order to get money he finally had to take measures which he had no right to take, but which were absolutely necessary. He thought it probable that there had been waste and confusion, but admitted he was beginning to be of the opinion that to some extent that was unavoidable.

This may or may not have made the Directors realize that, where the state of the Company's affairs in Upper Canada was concerned, Galt's alleged extravagance was not the only factor to be taken into account. However, it certainly suggests, as Galt later came to suspect, that Smith's role as an employee of the Company was not primarily that of accountant and cashier, but of investigator. In his capacity of accountant and cashier he should normally have reported whatever he found wanting or in need of overhaul at Guelph or at the Company's York office, in the first instance, not to the Directors, but to Galt as the Company's duly appointed representative in Upper Canada. It does seem highly probable that an arrangement existed between Smith and the Directors whereby he was or considered himself to be answerable to them only, and could thus with impunity bypass Galt's authority.

Galt assumed, as we learn from his letter to the Directors dated September 25, 1828, at Guelph, that Smith, when he arrived, would have directions for providing funds, but in this he was mistaken and consequently found that he must either apply to personal friends for money or stop payment. His duty to the Company obliged him to adopt the former course. The bank, he reported, had that morning refused a cheque for £27 and when he asked the reason had been told that no cheque bearing his signature would be paid. He wrote the Directors again on October 1 from Guelph to tell them about the awkwardness of no funds being available. He was certain that the Bank had misinterpreted its orders. There was nothing definite to report from Goderich, he informed them on October 13. Owing to the sickliness of the season, some of the Company's men, including Prior and Dunlop, were ill with ague and fever. He had advertized for but been unable to hire a doctor; there was no quinine and it was difficult to get provisions. The value of land was so greatly regulated by its accessibility that no general rule as to price could be laid down. Everything depended upon roads. Want of proper accommodation for both his business and himself had been submitted to until the inconvenience had become a considerable aggravation. He had nevertheless found both anxiety and hardship diminished and his work falling into a smoother current since coming so much nearer to the actual scene of operations. By his next letter from York on October 25 he told them that Thomson, the clerk and two other employees failed to give satisfaction and had been dismissed.

The last straw was Smith's behaviour in connection with the levee which, at Maitland's invitation, Galt attended at York at the beginning of November 1828, to be introduced to Sir John Colborne, the new Lieutenant-Governor. When Galt got back from the levee Smith confronted him and bursting into a frenzy said that Galt should have taken him "in" his "hand" when he went to the ceremony. There was something in Smith's attitude, Galt observed, resembling a threat of complaining to the Directors and implying that Smith had a sort of authorized surveillance over him. The situation, Galt concluded, had become unbearable. He was seriously considering going back to England when he heard that Smith had crossed Lake Ontario. [15]

On November 5, Galt posted a brief report to the Directors in which he stated that he was prepared to undertake whatever they desired and asked whether Smith's reports were to be forwarded without passing through his hands. Smith wrote to him from York on November 5 protesting that, after being four months in the province, all he had found in the way of records kept by Galt was an incomplete register of sales. There was no general cash book or ledger, he asserted, though Galt both verbally and in writing had promised to produce them; and, furthermore, in direct breech of faith with him and contrary to the Court's instructions, Galt had submitted his reports privately to the Directors. He also informed Galt that he was preparing to leave for England. On the same date the Directors addressed a sharp note to Galt charging him with always vindicating what was past instead of making computations as to probable future expenditures. No funds for general purposes, they said, would be made available to him till he complied with their request for specific estimates and requisitions for future outlays. They charged him in addition with devoting more time to discussing his personal affairs than to providing particulars concerning sales of land. What money, they wanted to know, had been spent, and what remained? No answer would be forthcoming to his repeated requests till information had been sought from the bank itself. Some money would be allowed, but only for salaries and allowances. The letter was signed by Easthope.

Galt notified the Directors on November 9 that, in order to get certain misconceptions cleared up and the Company's business put on a proper footing, he had made up his mind to return to London. He would not be

121

able to be with the Court before its December meeting, but the meeting could be adjourned. A week later he reported Smith's "clandestine departure" to the Directors, at the same time drawing their attention to the problems which he had been left to contend with. Having had to draw on funds paid into the office to meet essentials, he suggested that the deficit be made up by the withholding of his salary. Since the injury to his eyes, he had been in need of a better clerk; he would like the general state of affairs to be looked into by independent investigators; and, as he noted in the *Autobiography,* considering the position in which he had been placed by Smith's "precipitate flight," he could not "without a scandalous abandonment of duty" go just yet to England; he was faced with the task of making up the accounts which Smith had left in a worse state than they were in when he took charge of them.[16] It was his firm belief, he went on to say in his letter of the 16th, that Smith imputed blame before having facts to go upon, assumed that great faults had been committed in the management of the Company's affairs, and made accusations about meddling in politics, irreverence toward the Governor, and other misdemeanours. All the accusations were shown, on investigation, to be destitute of truth. Smith could not stand opposition; his manner was imperious; he got worked up easily; had made, then retracted, a statement to the effect that he was acting on authority from Hullet and McGill. He was irascible with the settlers, had given trouble with regard to Thomson's negligence, and when the conduct of the clerks came to be investigated, he shrank from taking his full share of responsibility, though himself one of the causes of the investigation. Nevertheless, feeling the humiliation of the financial state of affairs, and agreeing that something must be done, he had gone to York and made arrangements with the bank, whereby a stop was put to the rumour which had reached as far as Niagara, that "the bubble of the Canada Company was burst." Galt followed this up with a letter to the Directors on November 17 in which he complained that a bill for £100 had been protested, and deplored this "wreck of the Company's credit."

In his next letter to the Directors of November 27 he refuted certain allegations Smith had made. He denied that Smith had not been furnished, as asserted, with particulars; Smith was "self-sufficient" and ignorant of routine procedures; "lost time in meddling with" what was no concern of his, "fluttering from one thing to another as if bustle were business" and was "a great theoretical political economist." Instead of sticking to the sensible procedure whereby company employees got less in summer, and more than their stated pay in winter, because then they needed more, he, in his interfering fashion, paid them the flat rate for the summer months with the result that, come winter, they were going about begging necessities for their families. He could not get it into his head that he was dealing with a type of person who would take every advantage; and talked as if he expected to find men as uniform in character and disposition and as consistent as arithmetical figures; he had carped about the management of the stores and alleged the entering of imaginary names on the map of the Guelph settlement. Security, however, was obtained for every item issued and maps conformed with legal requirements. By what authority or knowledge did Smith claim the right to judge where expenditure on the Priory was concerned or keep insisting that the head office of the Company should be at York instead of Guelph? With existing ample facilities for easy access by road to Guelph, there was nothing to complain of as regards the main office of the Company being situated there.

Smith reached London on December 8, 1828 and wrote immediately to the Directors. He made out that owing to the lack of business methods and of order and regularity in the keeping of accounts in the Company's operation in Upper Canada, it was impossible for him to account for how things stood. That was why, he said, he had come home. He regretted having failed in his mission. The Directors gave Galt notice on December 11 of Smith's arrival, and that his report would be considered by the Court at its December 18 meeting.

In submitting the accounts of the Guelph settlement to the Directors on December 13, 1828, Galt stated that official arrears were less than he had feared in his anxiety; on December 21 he advised them that an arrangement had been reached with the bank at York to meet the situation; for fifteen days of a six weeks period, he informed them on Christmas Eve, he had been on horseback in bad weather and on poor roads. On December 30, he told them that the only way out he could think of was to get credit from New York. There was the thousand pounds per annum of his salary he had left in the Company's hands so that, in the event of his drawing on them, they might be secured against any possible loss. Smith in London wrote to the Directors on December 27, admitting that he could not produce all the vouchers for sums expended in Upper Canada. He had left them behind in the haste of his departure; he was mortified and deeply hurt by his negligence.

With a feeling of finality in everything he did, Galt made up his mind to go by sleigh through the forest road and visit the Goderich settlement. While he made preparations, he reflected that his employment as superintendent of the Canada Company, though not unmixed with troubles, was congenial enough. His tasks were so evidently calculated to relieve the mass of human sufferings, that, irksome at times though the performance of them might be, it was possible to take great delight in contemplating them. He earned a respectable salary, but money matters were not, never had been, the chief object of his thoughts. If for a fleeting moment he was thinking of them now, it was because of the remembrance of his children and his concern for what might become of them.

As he travelled to Goderich, snow began falling heavily and often reached impassable heights in the glades of the new road, so that the sleighs were obliged to deviate into the woods. At times the travellers lost their way. On one of these occasions they halted to consider whether they should proceed or wait for daybreak. However, the arrival of teams with provisions showed that they were going in the right direction, so they pushed on and presently reached one of the receiving houses where they stopped over for the night.

On arriving at Goderich Galt put up at the log house in which, after landing from the *Bee* at the time of the exploring expedition, he had stayed with Dr. Dunlop. The land was wreathed in snow and Lake Huron covered with ice as far as the eye could see. The place selected for the new town had undergone a transformation, a large part of it having been cleared and several houses built.

Next day the wind blew so violently that he had to remain indoors. The following morning which was bright and calm he spent viewing the surroundings and the progress that had been made. He left nothing unexamined, but his observations were made in a cursory fashion and with a sense of listlessness. It vexed him to think that not only had the Canada Company originated in his suggestions, and been established by his endeavours in disregard of many obstacles, but that he had contrived a system which, though extensive and complicated, could be managed easily; yet for no fault he had committed, he was destined to reap from it only troubles and vexations, and something which he felt to be an effort to disgrace him.

One thing rankled in particular. The Huron Tract, nearly sixteen hundred square miles in extent, was divided into townships. Most of these had been named after the Directors, with three or four that were left over named for men in office. There was no objecting to that, but why had he been passed over? It was one of those things that the Directors were best able to explain. Well, he was content with having formed the Company, not being the first parent that has had unfilial offspring.

It would not have mattered so much if the Company had been one of those sordid undertakings the sole object of which was monetary gain; but considering that it was fraught with benevolence, calculated to assuage distress in the mother country, and improve the condition of those forced thereby to emigrate, he was sorry to see it sunk into a mere land-jobbing huckstery, and abortive of almost all the promises by which the government was induced to part with the lands.

His visit ended, he set out on the return journey to Guelph. It was more than adieu to Lake Huron; it was a last farewell, for he considered that, from the moment he lost sight of its lonely shores, his connection with the Company was closed.[17]

On January 2, 1829 Fullarton informed Galt on behalf of the Court of Directors that with reference to his letters of November 16, 17 and 22, and in view of a report from the Committee of Treasury and Accounts, the Court at its meeting on January 2 had considered it expedient to "recall" him from the management of the Company's concerns in Canada and that he regretted to have to announce to him that he was recalled accordingly. It was the intention of the Court that his successor should be the bearer of the Court's resolution which, however, would not be transmitted till the appointment of his successor had taken place. The Directors wrote Galt a little later intimating the appointment of Thomas Mercer Jones to take over entirely from him and to be associated with a gentleman in the province – William Allan, it transpired – in carrying on the Company's work. At the same time they wrote to Jones authorizing him to take charge and advising him that in any difficulty he should apply to the Attorney General of Upper Canada.

Galt must have felt very keenly, as he put it in a letter of January 10, the "absconding" of William Gilkinson's eldest son, David who abruptly left the employment of the Canada Company which Galt had procured for him, to work at Flamboro with one of his father's business acquaintances. Galt had another bout of illness and, since he could not hold a pen, Reid, his assistant, had to handle his correspondence. At the beginning of February, when he was himself again, he forwarded to London a report he had got Joseph Fellows, the sub-agent of the Pulteney Land Company to prepare for submission to the Directors, and which concluded thus:

> Upon the whole, I beg leave most respectfully to state, to the Company my decided opinion that Mr. Galt's agency has been conducted with sound judgment, a proper regard to economy and the interests of the Company; that his proceedings have promoted their best interests; and, I believe, the Company cannot more effectually promote their own views than by delegating to him the most ample discretionary powers.[18]

What the Directors thought of the report "is not known," Galt remarked in a note appended to the full text of it, reproduced in the *Autobiography*. From the day he forwarded it till March 24, he had no despatches from London, but "many tokens of assurance that the Company would soon be broken up," which made his resolution to return to England seem more necessary than ever.[19]

On the morning of his departure, early in April, 1829, the settlers at Guelph assembled in front of the Priory and presented him with an address in which they expressed their gratitude for how he had treated them and their good wishes for his return. He left Guelph after breakfast, having given his servant instructions to go on ahead with his luggage to Albany. He proceeded to York in order to conclude one remaining item of business in connection with irregularities involving some of the clerks. While he was there, the Lieutenant-Governor had the kindness to write in favourable terms about him to the Secretary of State.[20]

There were none of the ceremonials that had heralded his arrival in Upper Canada, and no fanfares at his departure. Samuel Strickland paying tribute to the kindness and liberality with which Galt had treated him, was sorry to hear of his "retirement," and considered he had lost a true and affectionate friend. "I could not help, therefore," he wrote, "noticing with regret that, although most of the clerks belonging to the office were at that time in Toronto, only Dr. Dunlop, Mr. Reid, and myself accompanied Mr. Galt to the landing place to see him depart and cry 'God speed!'"[21] The London Directors, to their credit, paid Galt's passage home.

We can picture Galt standing at the stern-rail of the vessel that bore him across Lake Ontario, to what he knew not lay ahead, watching the figures of those three, Dunlop and Strickland in particular, who had stood by him through thick and thin, dwindling gradually in the distance, until finally they disappeared from sight.

Galt's wife wrote to her aunt from Guelph on April 1st, 1829:

> Mr. Galt being obliged to go home, I take the opportunity of writing you. I intend taking Robina[22] with me to Chambly where my dear boys are at school and I mean to remain there till Mr. Galt returns but it is doubtful to me if he will return. You may remember a dream which I had and told you . . . of Mr. Smith: you observed Mr. Smith is acting under a cloak; this has truly been verified; it is owing to the conduct of Mr. Smith that Mr. Galt has to go home and it will not be for lack of endeavour on Smith's part if Mr. Galt loses his situation...

In the later stages of the correspondence passing between Galt and the

Directors the possibility of relations being broken off between them was becoming increasingly evident, but it reflected rather badly on the Directors that, when the break came, Galt was so harshly dealt with. Being recalled was for Galt a wound that went much deeper than, at the time, his customary reticence would allow him to reveal. Was it, then, necessary for the Directors to rub salt into the wound, by arranging for Galt's successor to serve him with formal notice of his being superseded? Galt did not in fact receive such notice before leaving Canada. Thomas Mercer Jones reached York on April 19, but by then Galt was on a ship bound from New York to Liverpool. As for Galt's wife and family, because of uncertainty as to whether his recall was intended to be final, he was allowed, he said, to leave them "in the woods of America."[23]

Chapter 8

END OF AN INTERLUDE

On May 20, 1829, Galt disembarked at Liverpool where he heard that the Company was to be broken up. On arrival in London he went to the Canada Company office, but, as the Court of Directors was not meeting that day, obtained no satisfaction.

Downie, one of the Directors and a Member of Parliament, whom he met next morning at breakfast, seemed to be of the opinion that Galt's dismissal was not final; he had simply been recalled by the will of the proprietors, and the Directors had had no choice but to obey. Galt was perplexed by Downie's view of the situation, but decided to enquire no further till the day appointed for a meeting of the Court.

His reception when it did meet was in no way remarkable, except for his mentioning the strangeness of their thinking of such a disparaging measure as an abrupt dismissal while in receipt of the letter intimating his intention to come home. One of their number, an old friend of his, made an observation which seemed to suggest that the letter had been overlooked because of the circumstances in which it had been received. Nothing further was said, however, as to whether this was so or not. Galt decided then to attend a forthcoming meeting of the proprietors so that, if blame were attached to him, he would be in a position to vindicate himself.[1]

He wrote to Blackwood on May 29 as follows:

You have heard what has happened in the Canada Company. The capital is not forthcoming and the *actual* shareholders have intimated the fact to Government . . . the true state of money matters will show that another cause than my alleged obstinacy was working to the effect that has now taken place.

My stay in London, and on this side of the Atlantic, will not perhaps be longer than three or four months.

On June 17 he wrote again to Blackwood to report what had by then transpired. The general meeting of the Company, he said,

> took place on Friday and towards me was kindly enough. It is the state of money matters on the part of the proprietory that is the root of all the evil which brought me home – I had expected war with the Directors, but on the contrary they appear friendly towards me and if they can get the Government to modify the contract to the altered state of the Company's finances it is not unlikely that I may be requested to resume my function.

Galt's hope of being able to resume his duties was no mere pipedream on his part, because the Court of Directors at their meeting in January 1829 had resolved to recall him and select a suitable person to replace him temporarily. They also wanted to decide what to do with Smith. Furthermore, according to the January resolution of the Court, no judgement was to be given until Galt was heard, if there was to be a hearing.

In a letter to Moir on July 14 Galt wrote:

> The truth has come out. It was not alleged headstrongness on my part that has been the cause of what has taken place, but the want of funds to carry into effect the operations in the manner originally proposed by me, and to which the Government was so reluctantly brought to accede – It was a weak policy to seek for fault in my proceedings, when the reduction of my emoluments was found to be indispensable, but the same policy has been acted upon, I understand, towards Dr. Dunlop. He was recalled on the pretext of some political indiscretion: but the sentence has been revised, and he has since been placed on the better footing of being served with a notice to quit, on account of the necessity to economize.
>
> I have heard no literary news since my return, being engaged in wading through the Company's accounts . . . My arrangements on leaving Canada were for my being back early in October: but that is now out of the question; nor indeed would I go again in the Companys (sic) service without more discretionary powers being allowed me. The attempt to manage so complicated a concern by instructions from London was too absurd.

It was disingenuous toward him on the part of the shareholders, as he said in a further letter of June 30 to Blackwood, to complain of a fault which the terms of the contract obliged him to commit, if following up the original views and intentions with which the Company was formed could be imputed as a fault. We also learn from this letter that Dunlop had not been dismissed but only told that he could no longer be allowed the salary at which he had been engaged.

Meantime Galt had learned from private sources that negotiations were afoot to have the government take back the Company's lands. He suspected certain parties might step in and buy up, but by some skilful lobbying in high places he managed to prevent this. As a result, the proprietors had reason to be thankful that "instead of gloating and chuckling over their high priced stock, they were not seen later going about the Stock Exchange with their eyes watering and their fingers in their mouths."[2]

Up to this point, despite all he had been through, Galt is still the "bonnie fechter," knocked down one minute, up on his feet and ready to go in again the next, or, like Mr. Pawkie in *The Provost,* buttoning his coat the tighter about him and looking out "the crooser [more spiritedly] to the blast"; but "the natural effects of" his "recall" began to manifest themselves in, among other things, his being dunned for debt. It was rumoured that he was on the eve of returning to Canada and this brought upon him every person who had a claim on him, direct or indirect, awaiting settlement. Having left authority with the accountant of the Canada Company to receive payment of a thousand pounds a year of his salary to discharge certain accounts on his behalf, he had drawn on the accountant for a half-yearly payment to defray the cost of the education of his three sons when they were at school in Reading with the well-known Reverend Dr. Valpy, a classical scholar of high repute. Galt had sent the bill to the Canada Company accountant to be transmitted, when accepted, to Dr. Valpy, but this had not been done.[3]

On receipt of a note from Valpy demanding payment, Galt begged his indulgence which he thought he might ask of him, considering that Valpy was not only a personal friend of twenty-five years standing, but had been for about forty years a partner of Dr. Tilloch. The answer was a formal demand for payment from Valpy's solicitors.

Galt calculated that, independent of a security given for his chief debt and several farms in Canada sufficient for the others, he was embarrassed to no more than the extent of the arrears on an annuity of £300 which, although irregularly paid, he had long counted on. He appeased his pride by the knowledge that he had always made more than he expended and that the only reason for his ever having been in financial difficulties was other people's failure to fulfil their obligations to him.

On July 6, 1829, he informed Blackwood that he had executed an assignment of his property, preparatory to availing himself of the Insolvent Act, should he be forced to it. In reviewing his affairs from 1819, it appeared he had received upwards of £19,000 in money, and had he not meddled with shares and discounted bills, he should have had, at the time of writing, about £9,000. He had about £2,000 worth of property nearly the whole of which was in Canada, a great part of it in land, but it could not be realized easily and he had never meant to sell it. To have avoided the crisis he should have had to raise £1,100, an impossibility. The only course open to him was to recover freedom of action as quickly as possible.

When the writ served on him by Valpy's solicitors was returnable, he prepared himself to surrender. Before doing so, however, he entreated Valpy to relent in his proceedings. Valpy did not relent. Galt had then no choice but to submit to the Insolvent Act and take refuge in the King's or Queen's Bench prison, the Commitment Book of which for 1828-1830 contained the following entry:

1848. John Galt, Rend. etc. 15th July 1829 in discharge of his Bail at the suit of the Reverend Richard Valpy D.D. Oath £197.14.8 and was thereupon commd. By I. Littledale.
Dis. 10th Nov. 1829 u. Insolvent Act.

In a work dealing with the London prisons Hepworth Dixon wrote:

Who has not heard of Queen's Bench prison? Who, that has come to years of discretion, and inherited that 'right of man,' the privilege of going to gaol for his own debts, has not more than heard of it? Is there a lounger in Pall-Mall, a saunterer in Regent-street, who has not had a friend there at one time of his life or another? . . . In fact, where is the statesman, poet, artist, noble, wit, politician, or philosopher, who has not paid a visit to its secluded courts – taken momentary shelter from the storms of life within its peaceful haven – and gathered there new strength to contend against a wasteful world? . . . No one, indeed, but knows thee well – perhaps too well; for thou art truly not so bright, curious, picturesque, as the imagination paints thee. The pencil of Haydon and the pen of Fielding have shed a glory round thee which is not thy own. In truth, genius has dealt with thee too graciously. So many rays from the luminous track of our country's literature have fallen on thy walls and courts, we hardly think of thee as the dark and loathsome thing thou art. The foreign splendours rest upon thee as a veil: but in truth it is the veil of Mokannah – hiding a very hideous thing beneath.[4]

We are left to imagine the sense of "indescribable humiliation" Galt experienced as he was led through the main gate in the fifty foot high brick wall of this formidable institution and found himself lodged in the cell, where, cut off from former acquaintances as he intended he should be, he applied himself resolutely to the task of building a new scheme of life in which "the secondary condition of authorship was . . . made primary."[5] We are also left to guess at what was going on around him during his imprisonment. In his letters to Blackwood at this time, he gave "London" – nothing more – as his address; and impressed on Blackwood his desire that no one should know of his situation which he referred to as "managing" his "affairs." His old friend Prince Koslovsky visited him in prison, was astonished to find him there, and insisted on buying him out. Galt was grateful, but declined, insisting that until the debt was paid, the moral obligation could never be removed. On October 30, 1829, he promised Blackwood he would soon be sending him his new address, and on November 28 that he had got his "affairs all settled."

Why was Valpy so intractable, one wonders, so pressing in his demands? Was he so desperate for money that he could not wait until Galt realized his assets in Canada? To go by what is known of the alacrity with which the Canada Company was made over into a Family Compact concern, after the severance of Galt's connection with it in Upper Canada, it is evident that the possibility of Galt's returning to resume his functions there had at all costs to be forestalled in the interests of the Compact.

"The transplanting of the British system of government," we are told, "involved not necessarily the creation of a State Church in the colonies, but the maintenance of an intimate connection between the Established Church in England and the colonial administration."[6] Was Valpy made or did he offer himself as a tool in the Family Compact's hands? There could be reason to suspect so, and, if in fact he was, the swiftness and relentlessness of his action against Galt is less hard to understand. From the day of the latter's arrival back in London to the date of his committal to the King's Bench prison, less than eight weeks elapsed, and one suspects, before any favourable impression he had made on the Canada Company's London Directors could take effect, before he should be in a position to extricate himself, it was felt that he must be got out of the way. Be that as it may, purely in terms of the close relationship that had long existed between them, Galt, at the time, felt very bitter about the way in which Valpy had acted; later, however, he forgave him.

Galt also had a defamatory charge brought against him by a clerk whom he had dismissed for embezzling Company funds in Upper Canada, but had refrained from prosecuting to avoid giving the Family Compact further occasion to complain. He found it difficult to attach much credibility to a report in one of the Canadian newspapers that in the charge brought by the clerk political or party feeling was involved. It is not, however, entirely without significance that the clerk was a relative of Robinson, then Surveyor-General of Upper Canada and one of the Family Compact.

Smith, the accountant, likewise had come into the picture with a pamphlet which he published against Galt and to which Galt replied with a mass of supporting testimony from Anthony Van Egmond, Dunlop, T. B. Husband the clerk, and Prior the overseer, of the Guelph settlement, and Joseph Fellows the sub-agent of the Pulteney Land Company. Van Egmond delivered the *coup de grâce* by his plainspoken assertion that the Canada Company's credit had been

> brought to *Zero* by the deceptif *fanfaronnados* of Thomas Schmith, Esq., – by having often a little pile of silver dollars, and a few gold pieces, laying on the writing-table in his office; telling stories, as if he had all the treasures of the East at his command; and paying but a very few, or none at all; and by giving orders, who made laugh all the men of sense who heard of them, and made the Company to a set of – I wont say what.[7]

In a long wheedling letter of January 15, 1829, Smith attempted to ingratiate himself with the London Directors of the Company, at the same time insinuating that he would be the very man to fill Galt's shoes. He got short shrift for his pains. The Directors informed him on January 24, that, on six months' notice from the date of their communication, his appointment was terminated, since it was not considered expedient to renew his mission to Canada.[8]

Smith's appointment may have been terminated simply on account of the Company's need to economize but, if not, his competence must have been found wanting, and his dismissal could be taken as a tacit admission of Galt's being absolved of the charges Smith had made against him. Although they did not admit it, the Directors must have been well aware that Galt had been made a sort of scapegoat for a certain amount of administrative ineptitude for which they were responsible. Shortly before he was recalled, Galt's bills were ordered to be paid as they fell due. Although they were, in fact, paid by the Company, the bills were endorsed as unacceptable, a procedure which, Galt claimed, implied a doubt of his integrity and had the effect of seriously injuring him in Canada. He was greatly and, indeed, quite unnecessarily embarrassed by the Court of Director's unbusinesslike transactions with the Bank of Upper Canada, as may be seen from a letter dated February 5, 1829, which John Wenham, the president of the bank sent to the Directors. There was some wrangle between Wenham and Downie, representing the Court of Directors, over the interpretation of expressions and terms which the Directors had employed in making their arrangements with the bank. From the bank president's point of view the instructions had been anything but precisely and clearly defined, so far as concerned the business Galt had to transact for them.[9]

In spite of his imprisonment and other problems, Galt had managed to write two other novels (*Lawrie Todd* and *Bogle Corbet*). He contemplated emigrating if he could get a grant of land, and approached "Lord ———" who had always been extremely kind to him and requested him to speak to Sir George Murray, the Secretary of State. His Lordship, responding instantly, walked with him to see Murray at Downing Street. Nothing, however, came of it.

On one occasion Edward Ellice called and invited Galt to dinner. Galt was more than grateful for this, the first visit he received from any of his old acquaintances after his release from the King's Bench. He found his thoughts turning "into their former habitudes" and when there seemed to be no possible object to which they might be directed, he was engaged by Colburn and Bentley the publishers, to write the life of Byron. Then, through the good offices of Lockhart and Murray, the bookseller, he was appointed to the editorship of the *Courier*. The work did not prove so agreeable as he had fancied it would be, so, after a while, he gave it up. The fact was he was not well. R. P. Gillies, in his *Memoirs* deals at some length with the havoc wrought on Galt's health by his imprisonment.

Beginning "insensibly to shake off" his "drowse," he wrote for his family. Mrs. Galt and the boys had been on their own at Chambly in Lower Canada for the best part of a year, but were back in England by June 1830, as may be deduced from a letter Galt wrote to Moir from 29 Halfmoon Street, London some six weeks after their arrival. He also wrote to Moir on September 25th:

... I do not get well, but think I am somewhat improved, and I am inclined to resume the plan of life I formed before the Canada Co. – Mrs. Galt and I have had several conversations, and among others about Inveresk being our place of rest if we could find a place to our liking there – I have no capital but I can with health count on an income of at least £1,000 a year and if that will do I would again retire. – Give me your opinion freely. I am paying two hundred and fifty guineas for our house here, and I see that I might save a hundred – a great deal more if I took an unfurnished house.

Moir, it would seem, had no advice to offer on house prospects at Inveresk, or Galt and his wife may have abandoned the idea of going there, for they moved soon afterwards to Old Brompton in the London area and took up residence in Barn Cottage.[10]

The general state of Galt's health, after a visit to Cheltenham, and, in particular, the onset of the paralytic strokes which finally brought about his death, are dwelt on in the *Autobiography*: "I could, indeed, no longer," he wrote, "equivocate to myself that the noon of life was come, and the hour striking."[11]

For some time past his only interest had been literature, but his "constitutional bias for activity" at length reasserted itself and he began to look around for something to which he could more earnestly apply himself than to literary pursuits. Just then his attention was drawn to the marked improvement in the shares of the Canada Company and it struck him that a company organized on lines similar to the latter stood a good chance of success in Lower Canada. He went immediately to work on the idea and the outcome was the British American Land Company[12] which went into operation early in February 1832 and received its charter in 1834.[13] Galt was appointed Secretary but for health reasons had to resign in December 1832.

In mid-July of that year Galt made a further effort to revive his plan for a new colony in Lower Canada, on the basis of a tract of land, "distinct from what may be called the jurisdiction of Lower Canada," being assigned by the government, and sent a detailed statement on the subject to Earl Grey.[14] The plan was, however, as little favoured by Grey as it had been by Dalhousie, and Galt let the matter drop. During this period he also proposed a plan for establishing a Land Company in Nova Scotia but the government's Emigration Committee rejected it.

There was a sequel to Galt's colonizing schemes which he had not reckoned with – the departure of his three sons to Canada, John and Thomas early in 1833 and Alex at short notice in 1834.[15] John went to farm at Goderich where he later became Registrar of Huron County. Thomas put in six years at the Toronto headquarters of the Canada Company, then turned to the study of law in which he earned a knighthood as Chief Justice and as the foremost criminal jurist of his time in Upper Canada. Alex was nominated for a junior clerkship in the office of the British American Land Company at Sherbrooke in the Eastern Townships and rose to the position of Commissioner. His career will be fully dealt with in the second volume of this work.

Galt felt depressed and lonely at losing his three boys, as in truth he had, for their paths never crossed again. He was considerably heartened however, by a letter he received from the Earl of Dalhousie, part of which read as follows:

> Your Company has now brought a powerful machinery to work for the Public good, as well as their own, an energy which the Government was not able to create . . . I wish you success with all my heart . . . You have given proof of its effects in Upper Canada to admit of no doubt of its influence elsewhere.
>
> When in Canada I did doubt your success, because I doubted The Company would persevere in so great an outlay as was then proposed; but I only rejoice the more now, in the success of their perseverance . . . Allow me to repeat my cordial wishes that the Canadas and The Company may equally benefit in the great undertaking . . . Wherever I go, I shall always entertain that esteem and regard for you, which began and grew in our acquaintance in Canada, and in these feelings Believe me to remain
>
> faithfully yours
Dalhousie
>
> John Galt, Esq.[16]

From August, 1833, onward Galt's health was steadily deteriorating, as we learn from his letters to Blackwood. The paralysis was leaving his body and had gone more into his feet; he had had nine more strokes. The doctors had given it as their opinion, after a surgical examination, that the seat of his "most anomalous" disease was in the spine. The strength of his limbs was gone.

He rallied somewhat, for once again he took it into his head to go abroad. However, when he was on the point of leaving he did not have the strength to get his packing done in time. This was followed by a relapse. His situation, he wrote on February 3, 1834, to his sister in Greenock, had "arrived at the upshot." He was afraid that it might not be in his power to go overseas, as he had been very ill and had had to go to bed. Alexander's nomination for a clerkship had, however, strengthened his intention. It was not that he wanted the power of coming calmly down the hill for surely in Canada he would feel the change greater for there his situation was very different from what she imagined. He had had there a great trust and £2,000 a year, and she did him injustice in thinking he was actuated by any other feeling than the wish to be cheaper. He begged the feelings of a father.

What "the wish to be cheaper" refers to is not clear, but he proposed to stay for a short time with his sister and to leave from the Clyde when the London house was vacated. Mrs. Galt would be going to see her friends:

afterwards they would rendezvous at Greenock. He assured her that he was more resigned to his blighted life than she gave him credit for but still he frankly confessed that now and then he did repine which he acknowledged was very silly. Since it had been known that he intended to go abroad some of his friends had been very kind.[17]

On medical advice, he had to lie on his back, and in that position kept working hard at the *Literary Life*. He was concerned that it should exhibit what he was and show that he had reason for regarding his literary endeavours as secondary compared with other things, his colonial system in particular, which although only partly adopted, and irrespective of how it may have turned out for himself, he really considered an achievement.

To this period in his life belong those fairly frequent begging letters that he wrote to his publishers in his increasingly fruitless efforts to maintain a footing in the literary world for the sake of his bread and butter. He was, about this time, however, greatly heartened by the news that although his political opinions were well-known and although the government adhered to its resolution not to concede what he conceived to be his claims, it had admitted that, if he pleased, he might draw £200 to account on the Treasury, the amount of the provision made for him, however, not yet being fixed. "Being a Tory, as you know," he wrote to Prince Koslovsky, "I confess this liberality from Whigs was not expected."[18] He was evidently under the impression that this would take the form of an annuity, for he told Blackwood that he had received the first instalment within two days of learning about the government's intention. Nothing, however, came of that either, nor of the pension for which he was recommended by the King, though the latter, according to Moir, in virtue of Galt's writings having enhanced the country's literary reputation, gave him a present of £200 and permission to dedicate the *Literary Life* to him.[19] A somewhat belated gesture of generosity also came from St. Helen's Place, but, as Galt related to Lockhart in July, 1836, ". . . when I heard the Company, before I left London, were planning to vote me a sum of money, I wrote to the Court of Directors that I would not receive it."

Dr. A. T. Thomson, Galt's physician suggested that what he needed as a pick-me-up was a voyage or a holiday at the seaside. This may have partly been the reason for his decision to go to Greenock to feel the tangy breezes of the Clyde coast about him once again and rest up in the house at the corner of Blackhall and West Burn Streets, which, his sister had occupied, since the death of his father and mother. At the same time his situation in a financial sense, had, indeed "arrived at the upshot," for, as he confessed in a letter he wrote to Lockhart, "had I not done an act of justice to my sister many years ago when my hopes were perhaps different, I would be in absolute beggary.[20] She however is enabled to give me my father's house, generously allows me the half of her income and has advanced for me and my boys better than a thousand pounds."

The Galts vacated Barn Cottage on March 25, 1834, but their plans were upset somewhat by a recurrence of Galt's illness. On April 10, his wife wrote from 12 Cecil Street, Strand, to Blackwood (addressing him as "Will") to say that her husband had been ready to go to Scotland, but on the previous Monday morning had suffered another slight shock which had since confined him to bed, but he still trusted to be with Blackwood in the forthcoming week by which time he hoped that a severe internal pain would be abated. Galt himself writing to Blackwood some weeks later mentioned that he had had "another aggravation"; but at last the Galts were on their way north with a stop over at Edinburgh, as planned. Galt was disappointed at not being able to visit Blackwood after all, because the latter was seriously ill. His disappointment was, however, somewhat mitigated by a brief but warm-hearted letter from the Earl of Dalhousie expressing the hope that the strength of his constitution would surmount the tendency to the shocks from which he had been suffering, and intimating Dalhousie's intention of visiting him in Edinburgh some day during the following week.[21] Galt and his family were in Greenock by mid August, but for a while after their arrival he felt unsettled there. Writing to Moir on August 21, 1834 he mentioned that, finding his sister's house and garden so surrounded by buildings, as to preclude his taking the air, he had moved to Maybank, Gourock (some way up the coast), though his address would still be Greenock.

Over the next eighteen months he was – no new thing for him – beset with financial difficulties. On November 13, 1834, John Perry, the Secretary of the Canada Company in London, wrote to advise him that the Court of Directors felt confident "that *upon any proper adjustment of*" his "*Account, it would be found*" that he was "*greatly indebted to the company*"; also that the Court had "hitherto refrained from taking any legal measures for the recovery of" his "debt."[22] This communication "filled" Galt "with consternation," as he said in his reply of November 18 to the Directors. Apparently the debt for which he was held accountable had to do with certain items in his accounts while he was acting as the Company's superintendent in Upper Canada and with the vouchers left behind there by Smith. In the course of correspondence with the Directors on the subject, Galt had requested to be allowed to arrange the objectionable items with the Company's accountant, and afterwards submit to their own lawyer a case as to whether he was liable for these items. The accounts, he believed, were square, except for a small balance in his favour.[23] His request was, however, turned down by the Directors as their letter of November 13 clearly indicated. So far as is known, no further action was taken by them. The matter was either dropped or automatically terminated at Galt's death in April 1839.

Another financial problem of a private and a still more serious nature is alluded to in Galt's correspondence with J. G. Lockhart, to whom he wrote as follows in 1836:

> Without troubling you with a curious *secret* history the endeavour which I have long made to struggle with fate begins to yield and you can think for yourself what it may have for more than twenty years been, when I simply enumerate a few circumstances. At my marriage an annuity was settled with a reversion to my wife of 300 pounds per annum. In the first Quarter I had a fearful suspicion it was a vain show, and for many years it has proved entirely baseless. Mrs. Galt was advised to sell the security, by which my children were rendered penniless. The failure lately of her father's executor has brought all to light, and even after my death she is left without provision . . .
>
> The settlements on my wife should have brought her six hundred a year but they were formed in some delusion & the executor has failed by gambling on the Stock Exchange, and it turns out never invested, as directed, in public securities the assets he had received.

Mrs. Galt's letter of December 26, 1836 to Miss Tilloch from Greenock confirmed what had transpired. "I take," she said, "the opportunity of writing . . . to tell you that we have heard from Mr. Wilkinson (the executor) that the 2 Shares of the Star which were Mr. Galt's & mine by the marriage settlement are not included in the money which Mr. Wilkinson has rendered an account of – they are entirely lost."

During the period within which these financial problems arose Galt was writing off and on for the local *Advertizer*, his first two contributions being on the deepening of the Clyde, and on abuses connected with the passage of private bills through Parliament. These were followed by *A Review of the Report from Select Committee on Private Bill Fees, with Minutes of Evidence, A Legacy, To Glasgow and Greenock for the Improvement of the Clyde,* and a series entitled "Attacocus' Letters" in which the topics dealt with were "the Durham hobbleshow held in Glasgow"; the Reform issue; Whigs and Tories; triennial Parliaments; suggestions on the best method of remunerating the clergy; and a *Plan of Settling the Boundary Question with the Americans.*

Beginning with the May 7, 1835 issue of the *Advertizer* appeared a further series of articles devoted to Galt's latest "lucubrations" – "Description of Mr. Galt's Machine"; "Mr. Galt's Hydraulic Machine"; "Mr. Galt's River-Boat"; "Mr. Galt's Bellows-Boat"; "Mr. Galt's Piston Bark"; "Mr. Galt's Tidal Machine"; "A Substitute for Steam"; and "The Sea-Fed Engine for Propelling Vessels." Another of his schemes, reminiscent of what he had contemplated doing at one time in Upper Canada, was a plan for draining and selling the bogs of Ireland, "several influential patriotic gentlemen" having requested him to ascertain if a joint stock company could be formed for bringing this about.

Galt's correspondence with the *Advertizer* was, as he made out, meant to amuse his readers, and afford pastime for himself. It was intended just as likely to keep him in touch with reality – with the nearer outside world that lay immediately beyond the four walls of the room where he was now virtually a prisoner, and with that larger world beyond in which he had once moved. Maintaining any real contact with the outside world was wellnigh impossible, Greenock, as he once put it, being a "one-eyed place" and a "stupid place to get news."

It was much the same with him now as it had been when he had written to Moir from Barn Cottage about two years previously:

> The leaden slippers in which Time, . . . dawdles at the bedside of infirmity causes the invalid to become morbidly sharp sighted on the practices of the world. He soon sees the intervals lengthen in the visits of particular friends and feels himself the cause of more trouble to others than may be congenial to his own disposition. These observations, though they may seem to relate to trifles, are nevertheless serious things to him and make up a great part of the irksome burden of disease.

The only "particular friends" we know of, who in his last days visited him, were Miss Pigott, his former schoolfellow Alexander Rodger, and his Fullarton relatives. There were also a clergyman named Gilmour of a strongly Evangelical persuasion, whose main concern, one gathers, was to extract a death-bed confession from him; and the "man by trade a joiner," one of the two individuals without whose help Galt could not negotiate the stairs.

Miss Pigott described her first visit to Galt. She made her way up a dimly lit staircase, passing an open door leading to a tidily kept kitchen, and noted how the sharp-toned barkings of a faithful old black spaniel[24] caused a cleanly Highland girl, without shoes or stockings, to emerge from her scrubbing department to show her into a small room the windows of which looked onto a mean row of houses in a narrow street. Galt was sitting on a high-backed wheel-chair before a writing desk, with, on a small table beside him, two drawers, one containing neatly folded packets of manuscript papers, and the other his correspondents' recent letters. He was, as he then appeared to his visitor, "a type of the beginning and ending of human strength . . . it seemed as if all the . . . power of his . . . frame had taken refuge in his finely turned head . . .," she wrote.

Rodger, visiting him on November 7, 1835, found him sitting "with his feet far in within the fender," as he had been writing in another room, and his limbs had grown very cold. His sister, was in a sad state, Galt wrote to Mrs. Macnair; she was constantly in darkness (that is to say, she was blind) and he had heard her voice only once in seven months.

Archibald Fullarton was with his mother when she went to Greenock to visit the Galts in the fall of 1838, and left this account of the impression Galt made on him, he being then a boy of nine:

I remember the youthful awe with which I found myself sitting in a half-darkened room, opposite the, to me, large framed old gentleman with green shades over his eyes, sitting on a sofa or armchair in front of a table covered with green baize and conversing in quiet tones with my mother.[25]

From the notes the Reverend Gilmour kept of his visits,[26] we get some idea of the pitiful condition to which Galt and his sister had by this time been reduced. A few days before Galt died, he became extremely anxious to see his sister, who had long been confined to her bed from severe illness. He wanted to tell her how her many prayers for his personal interest had been answered. Her physicians objected to her being moved. Still, in the face of their remonstrances, she determined to see her dying brother. But when the appointed time came she was unequal to the trial and had to be returned to her sick bed. During one of the minister's visits Galt declared that he intended spending the summer in Ayrshire; but that was not to be.

The "noon of life was come," he had written prophetically, "and the hour striking." How soon, by the rapidity with which his health deteriorated after that, the "noon of life" was left behind, and it was that time at which, as the collect in the *Common Book of Prayer* has it, "the shadows lengthen, and the even comes, the busy world is hushed, the fever of life over and our work done." His friend Moir described his condition toward the end as "a state of waking dream." The dawn light of a May morning was just beginning to tip with light the uplands to the east of Greenock, and the first lark would be ascending with his joyous notes to greet the new-born day above the moors where, blithe and carefree, Galt had wandered as a boy, when he passed from this mortal life. The rising sun shone through the window of that room in his father's house where latterly he had known so much sadness, grief, and pain; but now there was only peace.

He was laid to rest in the old Inverkip Street burying ground that looks out now, as ever, on the blue waters of the Firth, with "the great black hills like sleeping kings" brooding eternally on the passing scene below – and away westward, by Kintyre and the Queen of the Hebrides, to the open sea – and beyond that, over the rim of the horizon, to the far land of his "philanthropic dream,"

Where lives his name, and men he planted there,
Long as the white oaks in lone distance stand,
The promised fullness of his vision share.[27]

*   *   *

Various reasons have been given for the eclipse of Galt's career in Canada. What stood between him and success, it is said somewhere, could only have been something in himself, most probably his habitual prickliness, his bull-at-a-gate methods, his not having the remotest notion of how to handle the bureaucracy. The facts do not bear out that this was the only thing, but it has to be admitted that it is one of the things that must be taken into account, especially in Galt's relations with the provincial government, more particularly in those areas where his words or actions laid him open to the suspicion that he engaged in political activities. Early in June 1827 he wrote to Maitland, the Lieutenant-Governor, to say how deeply he felt and how strongly he resented the imputation of his being a favourer of discontent and a meddler in politics, and that he would not allow to pass unnoticed "any repetition of the charge even by hypothetical construction." On December 26 of the same year he also wrote to Major Hillier, Maitland's secretary, drawing his attention to the fact that he had been told by the Directors of the Canada Company that as its superintendent he must not get mixed up in politics. Would the Lieutenant-Governor, in all deference to his "personal candour and public dignity," please inform him, he requested, whether: I. He had ever been prominent in politics as a political opponent, or an associate or instrument of political opponents; and, if so, what witnessess and proofs

143

were adduced in support of it; and II. He had done anything contrary to his duty toward the government.[28]

Galt's contacts with William Lyon Mackenzie and John Rolph were sufficient to lay him under suspicion of being "a favourer of discontent and a meddler in politics." The other faults imputed to him, if we are to take his word for it, of being "prominent in politics and a political opponent, or an associate or instrument of political opponents" of the government, were of a much more serious nature, and it was natural that he should take such an imputation, even "by hypothetical construction," seriously. Since then it has not only been suggested that there was nothing hypothetical about it, but positively asserted that he was one of the "prominent politicians," indeed one of the "agitators," in Upper Canada during the Maitland régime.[29] It is difficult to picture Galt in this somewhat lurid light or to be certain about whether the more serious charges which he claimed were laid against him were as real as he made them out to be; but supposing that William Lyon Mackenzie and John Rolph had never crossed his path, supposing that he had been quite beyond suspicion of being a "meddler in politics," he was, for the following reasons, due to circumstances not of his own making, caught up in the cross currents of provincial politics.

A Canadian historian has put forward the suggestion that "the point at which, more than any other, the Family Compact [in the usually accepted sense] may be said to have come into existence, . . . might reasonably be the end of General Hunter's administration in 1805, when an element among the public officials secured the selection of Alexander Grant as president and administrator of the province" (pending the appointment of Hunter's successor in office).[30] Grant who, with the rank of Commodore, had previously been in command of all British ships on the Great Lakes, has a special claim on our attention, for he forms a link with another family compact in the literal sense of the words. His third daughter married Thomas Dickson, the brother of William Dickson of Galt; a grand-daughter married Robert Nichol who, with Thomas Clark and Robert Grant enlisted Galt's services as agent for the war sufferers in Upper Canada; his fourth daughter married Galt's first cousin, William Gilkison, the founder of the Elora settlement. Nichol, Clark and the Dicksons to begin with were blood relatives. Even Robert Gourlay, William Lyon Mackenzie's predecessor as chief rabble-rouser in Upper Canada, also qualified for membership of this closely inter-related group, for his wife was connected by marriage with William Dickson and Clark.

Dickson, Clark and Nichol were all active in politics to the embarrassment of the Maitland administration. Dickson and Nichol were outspoken critics of the way in which land transactions and immigration were being handled by the government, and Strachan complained that opposition from Clark and Dickson would put people off leasing the Clergy reserves.[31] Galt was implicated in the turmoil of political life in the province from the moment he became involved in the claims for war losses. These were a sore point between Maitland and the claimants and it was contended by the reformists that those who clung to the coat-tails of the Family Compact stood to benefit most. Galt was evidently not aware that probably even before he arrived in Canada he was suspected of anti-Compact propensities and kept under surveillance by the Maitland administration. "If," Maitland wrote with unconcealed resentment, "you have read Mr. Galt's published tour thro' the Levant, no sneer or insinuation with respect to the Established Church or its ministers could surprise you."[32] Maitland and his advisers would hardly have overlooked Galt's connection with De Witt Clinton, the governor of New York State, who was "heartily disliked" by Simcoe "as a violent and able Antifederalist." Clinton "became widely known as the most radical of the Whig members" in the New York General Assembly, and his uncle, George Clinton, the "most distinguished representative" of the "radical Republicanism" that brought him "into conflict with Hamilton and Burr," was reputed to have had an agent or agents in Montreal to keep him informed of everything pertaining to British policy that transpired "in the heart of the enemy country."[33] Galt might protest that never in his whole life had he been a politician but there were circumstances, other than those already mentioned, which lent themselves to a somewhat different interpretation. His policy of attracting capitalists to the lands of the Canada Company would seem at first glance to be simply a matter of economics, but the statement made by him in his "Colonial Discontent"[34] that Upper Canada wanted "nothing more than a class of inhabitants whose circumstances and education would be such as to place them independent of the government, and enable them to act as a check both on the popular and official faction" rouses a suspicion that there were political implications in the policy he advocated after all.

Again, if he in fact got the idea into his head in founding the Guelph settlement "that it might be made, not merely a village or town, but a grand city, that might vie with York and become, some time or other, the seat of government,"[35] and if such a grandiose idea did get about the province, it is not surprising that the Canada Company got the name of being *imperium in imperio* (a kingdom within a kingdom). It was with this in mind that Maitland flatly stated that if Galt's temper and discretion were such as the Company desired to see exhibited by their managing agent, he would not say what the feelings and the situation of the members of the executive government in the colony must be, but they need not wonder if the people at least should soon be in doubt as to whether it was the government or the Company that they were bound in duty and interest to serve.[36]

Galt, it has been said, was often tactless when he could easily have adapted himself to the petty policies of the province without sacrificing any of his independence. Such self-adjustment to what Maitland's administration stood for was possible for some men, but not for Galt. In a letter to Blackwood the Edinburgh publisher, from London on July 30, 1821, he confessed to "the unsolemn effect that all pompous things had upon him." As he wrote in the *Autobiography*: "in proportion as a superiority is assumed, I have all my life risen against it . . . I am as well aware as any man can be that it sets up the hair on the backs of those who plume themselves on their birth or fortune."[37] He believed in the "divine right of resistance" to whatever presumed or attempted to tyrannize over the lives or thoughts of men. His quarrel with Maitland was the meeting of temperamentally irreconcilable opposites. He must have realized that in his differences with Maitland he was crossing swords with a man whose government "saw fit to countenance a one-sided persecution which was regarded as a form of despotism and which won for its victims an ill-deserved martyrdom."[38] That system had already broken individuals who came into open collision with it, and could be counted on to break him in the end.

The *Montreal Gazette* announced at the time of Galt's departure:

Mr. Galt the author who has hitherto acted as Manager for the Canada Company has been dismissed from his office by the Directors. Mr. Galt's character is unimpeachable, but it appears that he was too fond of having his own way, and this gave offence.

What really "gave offence" was that the Canada Company "in advertizing the country and attracting settlers contributed forcefully"[39] to the breakup of the closed system whereby the Family Compact ruled the roost. The latter were well pleased "to see the last of so vigorous and brilliant a competitor for power and influence in the colony"[40] as Galt who "with a freedom from class feeling characteristic of his own friends in Scotland, and unconscious of the spiritual significance attaching to 'old school ties,' disinterestedly carried on his work for the mere joy of doing something useful."[41]

The rock, it seems, on which Galt perished, from the standpoint of the Directors of the Canada Company aided and abetted by the accountant,

Smith, was his allegedly unwarranted expenditure and his bad management. To the first of these grounds for complaint against him, the trouble he had with the Directors was, however, not all due. A general business depression in England forced the shareholders and Directors of the Company to cut back on projects for which they had budgeted, when those projects were already well under way. In the controversy over improvements in the Company's territory in Upper Canada, which continued after Galt had gone, his successor, Thomas Mercer Jones, "received much undeserved blame," and acquired in the process

> a reputation for being a lazy man with little initiative, in spite of the fact that his difficulties largely stemmed from the shortage of money with which the directors were faced in developing the Huron area. Jones did lack an imaginative approach, but the directors could not escape responsibility for the situation as it evolved.[42]

There was also the matter of their get-rich-quick mentality. They considered, wrote Lawrence J. Burpee,

> that the first consideration was that the Company should pay dividends; the interests of the settlers were of only negligible importance. These points of view were so irreconcilable that the wonder is not so much that Galt and his directors finally came to the parting of the ways, as that he was able to stay long enough in Upper Canada to carry out most of his plans.[43]

Or, to quote Donald Carswell, "as the comfortable stay-at-homes who formed the Canada Company did not find the dividends coming in fast enough, they showed their Imperial spirit by dismissing their agent and cheating him of his money. Galt came back to England . . ." and "died at Greenock, the most 'devilishly unappreciated' great man of his own or any generation."[44]

As for Galt's alleged mismanagement, his "qualifications for such an important mercantile appointment"[45] as superintendent of the Company in Canada have been held up to criticism. "He was," says one critic, "a writer of note, the friend of poets, of novelists and of the most brilliant literary critics of the day; he had some training in business, and in law; but from what I can learn, he had had little experience as an organizer and administrator."[46] He "lacked the tact, the steadfastness and the efficiency to be an able administrator."[47] He "was simply not the man for the job."[48]

According to Strickland who was in a better position to judge, Galt evinced great cleverness as the original projector of the Canada Company, and afterwards displayed much judgement in the choice of the best situations for building towns and villages. Nevertheless, he committed some grievous mistakes. His ideas were generally good; but often not well carried out in detail. His first error arose in the selection of men to fill various offices belonging to the Company. Instead of appointing men of long experience in the country, and thus qualified practically to superintend workmen, he filled situations with unexperienced young men, newly arrived from home. Labourers were also for the most part new settlers, and were paid just as much as if they had been more experienced. If his appointments had been judicious, there was no doubt, to Strickland's way of thinking, that half of the outlay would have produced greater results.[49]

There are, of course, other favourable opinions. William Lyon Mackenzie affirmed after visiting Guelph that if Galt had been furnished with means, his plans, especially his bank, were in general calculated to be productive; that he doubtless expended a few thousand pounds uselessly, and paid two prices for many things; but what European, the "little rebel" asked, could have avoided doing so, if he expended money at all, in coming immediately from the home country to Canada.[50]

"The biggest problem," however, with the Canada Company's plans "went much deeper and was recognized by no one at the time. The opening up of the Huron Tract in 1829, when so much land was yet to be developed between it and the centres of civilization" – 1,300,000 acres, scattered in 200 acre lots across the 300 miles separating Kingston and Lake Huron – "was a mistake on the part of the Company. Their plans were premature. Consequently it probably would have been impossible to sink enough money into the scheme to make the experiment truly successful. For a Company that had almost given up because of financial hardship in 1829, it would certainly have been financial suicide."[51] Other problems existed with which Galt was left to contend as best he could. In the first place, as he wrote in the *Autobiography:*

> I overlooked my being the representative of others, who . . . were not
> . . . sufficiently acquainted with the difficulties to be overcome . . .
> responsible for the administration of nearly a million of money, I
> was hampered with the most inconsistent restrictions . . . I was not
> allowed to take with me any clerk, far less a person in whom I could
> confide; . . . In a word, I was left destitute of those resources of
> advice and information, which the nature of my mission so greatly
> required.[52]

The Directors from the outset denied him powers of agency for negotiating sales of land without prior consent from them. At the end of February 1827 he informed them that he was preparing a very full view of the

Company's property and the mean value of the lands in every township but still wanted leave to make contracts to complete sales instead of instructions for doing so. The Directors' response was that the reserves should be sold as opportunity offered without limitation to districts, and that he was to consider this expression of the wish of the Court as enlarging indefinitely his powers of sale so far as the reserves went, subject as before stated to ratification by the Court.

His transactions in this area were further complicated by the fact that unexpected competition was encountered from the commissioners appointed to dispose of the Clergy reserves and other lands, and that free grants of land continued to be made by the provincial government. According to Weir, Galt's transactions also encountered opposition from landed proprietors in the neighbourhood of York. In spite of all that, however, Galt "went ahead with his plans, and by sheer force of character and determination carried them through."[53] It was freely admitted by those in Upper Canada who could give an informed and unbiased opinion that he was tackling the land problem more energetically and more fruitfully than the Land Board of the executive had done. In his criticism of the policy of the executive, Charles Buller later on, in his work for the Durham Report, was to point by way of comparison to the delegation of the powers of government to a private company, that is to say, the Canada Company, resulting in more regular and rapid settlement on its lands than on those under the control of the officers of the Crown.

William Jerdan, a friend and literary contemporary of Galt, said of him that he

was a man of great activity of mind, extensive travel and prolific experience ... His splendid project for the allocation of lands and improvement of Upper Canada evinced the sagacity and comprehensiveness of a constructive and legislative faculty which is rarely met with even among the ablest and most experienced statesmen ... Richly gifted by nature, honest, diligent, and persevering, a course of worldly success might have been expected. It was ordered otherwise.[54]

In another writer's opinion he

combined the vision of the master planner with the qualities of an administrator ... He was not only an idealist, a dreamer, and a visionary, but a man of practical affairs, a man of drive, who got things done. He displayed initiative, enterprise and resource, the power of gripping situations and wresting the best results from them.[55]

He had, summed up O.D. Skelton,

> seen far and planned wisely . . . had conceived and carried through
> the organization of a company which at a stroke had doubled the
> revenues of the province and provided funds for much-needed
> development. His scheme of emigration brought to Canada some of
> the best stock that has ever gone to its making . . . If the Company in
> later days became a passive receiver of unearned increment and
> incurred the hostility of a large section of the province, the responsi-
> bility lay upon those who lacked the vision and the sympathy of the
> founder.[56]

The beneficial results of Galt's policy of attracting men of capital was
everywhere acknowledged, wrote Dunlop. Improvement had gone on in
a ratio so accelerated that in one year more was being done for the
advancement of the province than ten in former times would have accomplished.[57] Not so long after Galt had been cashiered, the benefit to the
Company he had confidently predicted started coming in; "shares rose in
value, the Company which owed everything to Galt re-established itself
at home and overseas; and from that day Galt's settlements have never
known a backset."[58] A special pamphlet was issued by the Canada Company from its London office in 1841, with the title, "A Statement of the
Satisfactory Results which have attended Emigration to Upper Canada
Comprising Statistical Tables, and other important information, communicated by respectable residents in the various townships of Upper
Canada with a General Map of the Province compiled for the Guidance
of Emigrants," and beginning: "The Canada Company in laying before
the public an analysis of their labours during the past twelve years, in
effecting the settlement of their lands in Canada, feel convinced that a
more gratifying spectacle than it presents, . . . has never been collected
before."

There follows a list of submissions from "well-found settlers" in various parts of the province. Nothing, it is said, "can be more gratifying or
triumphant than these interesting accounts." Then comes a reference to
"a body of settlers," who "a little more than ten years since, placed themselves on the Company's lands near Guelph," with "many instances of an
increase of capital in ten years seven fold, and other cases still more star-
tling and wonderful."

In a long eulogy of Huron County, the pamphlet mentions Goderich,
"surrounded by a country, whose fertility of soil is unsurpassed by any in
the Continent of America." Guelph, "in the neighbourhood of this
district," it is declared triumphantly,

originally belonged to the Company, and was settled by their instrumentality . . . it is now a district town, with four churches, numerous public buildings, . . . a large and increasing population, and is still progressing in wealth and importance . . .

The Company feel much satisfaction, that the advantages of Canada were first prominently brought before the notice of the people of the United Kingdom by their exertions; they are rejoiced to make public their success;

and so on and so forth. However, not once in all of the pamphlet's sixty pages is Galt as much as alluded to, far less given credit for any of the things on which "the Company" so nauseatingly and so smugly plumed itself. Galt has oftener been discredited by being wrongly identified with those "kings of the Canada Company" who came after him. They failed in so many ways to keep the trust he handed on to them. Their "management for many years was but a reflex of Family Compact sentiments, manners and government, despotic in matters social as well as business," and in exposing them for their alienation of lands to a whole host of people whose "vote and interest" they retained by the "glorious credit system," Galt gave expression to his conviction that from this cause alone the colony would be lost.[59]

This brings us to something that transcends although it was implicit in the work Galt did at the bidding of those who, from where they sat in St. Helen's Place, thought of themselves as moving him and Dunlop like the pieces on a chessboard. "Happy had it been for him," Katherine Thomson commented in giving us her penpicture of Galt, "had he followed the biddings of Nature, and brandished his pen only as the novelist or biographer! It served him in little stead when applied to the jobbings of a Company."[60] So far as his work in Canada is concerned, Galt, however, did not quite see himself in that light. He had much bigger game in view. The Canada Company, as a contemporary Canadian writer says. "was an opportunity to carry out the great dreams of colonization he had nursed for years,"[61] that "colonial experiment of great magnitude," as he himself conceived of it, "the best and greatest colonial project ever formed,"[62] which Jennie Aberdein is at pains to impress on us, "should never be forgotten by Canadians at least."[63]

The larger goal Galt set himself must first of all be seen against the background of the extent to which this country had developed before his work for the Canada Company began, and in the context of what he succeeded in doing for this country as part of that larger goal.

"Eighty years ago," as we read in a book published at Toronto in 1864,

151

Upper Canada was a wilderness from the Ottawa to the St. Clair. The first British settlements were made after the year of peace 1783, but previously to that date only a few insignificant and drooping French colonies lay scattered on the banks of the St. Lawrence, or grouped in remote isolation on the river Detroit . . . the province . . . was just emerging from the gloom of its forests. Over the whole of the most fertile and now most densely peopled western half, forest silence reigned, reigned undisturbed and supreme.[64]

"In 1782 . . . Upper Canada had barely 10,000 inhabitants . . . in 1824" – the year in which the provisional committee for the establishment of the Canada Company was formed – "the numbers had increased to 152,000, and in 1829" – when Galt was dismissed from the superintendency of the Company – "to 225,000".[65] These figures acquire significance from Burpee's appraisal of the situation, when he wrote:

To appreciate the place of John Galt in the pre-Confederation period of Canadian history one must remember what the Canada Company stood for in the story of Upper Canada, for it cannot be too forcibly said that John Galt *was* the Canada Company. One hundred years ago Toronto was the grubby little town of York; Hamilton and London were villages; the population of the entire province was only about one hundred and fifty thousand. Although eleven million acres, out of a total surveyed area of sixteen million, had been granted to individuals or set aside as Crown reserves, the growth of population had been very slow since the first influx of Loyalists, and there was nothing that could be dignified with the name of an immigration policy. John Galt gave Upper Canada such a policy.[66]

That policy applied to or included Lower Canada as well, for writing from Downing Street, London, to the Earl of Bathurst on March 9, 1824, Galt mentioned being informed by Wilmot Horton that the government had resolved to dispose of the Crown reserves in Canada in connection with a general measure that was intended to embrace the waste lands of all the North American colonies.

Potentially Galt's immigration policy did not stop short even at the boundaries of Canada. As C. E. Fryer says with regard to emigration from Great Britain:

The years after Waterloo saw no great rush from Britain. Indeed, until 1830, the numbers of British emigrants were not conspicuously greater than in the later eighteenth century, but British North America was the usual goal, . . . Perhaps the happiest episode of the period, although not for its hero, was the founding of the Canada Land Company in 1824 – 26, and the efforts of John Galt, on the spot, to make the great Huron grant a model colony. Galt's reputation as a pioneer has suffered, partly through his greater fame as a writer, partly through his inability to propitiate conventional officials and economical directors, but there were few qualities of the practical colonizer, save the gift of advertizement, and the power of attracting social influence, in which he was not easily Edward Gibbon Wakefield's superior. Guelph, Goderich and the towns of Western Ontario owed more to him than Adelaide and Wellington to the other.[67]

Well might Horton, with Canada as well as the larger view of things in mind, write to Bathurst on April 20, 1827, describing "this Emigration" as "a subject of primary national importance."[68]

Unlike our Fathers of Confederation who "builded better than they knew," Galt knew how well he had built. "When my numerous books are forgotten," he said in *The Literary Life,* "I shall yet be remembered – I contrived the Canada Company, which will hereafter be spoken of among the eras of a nation destined to greatness." He is remembered, however, and deserves to be, for a great deal more than that. It is said of him that in less than three years he performed prodigies of enterprise that entitled him to be regarded as the Father of the Eldest Dominion; that more than any other man he was responsible for the development of Canada; and that he ranks high among those who prepared the ground for Confederation. It is also said of him that his greatest achievements were as an Empire builder; that he is one of the significant figures in the making of the British Empire in the nineteenth century; and one of the first to develop the whole colonial idea.[69]

A trifle despondently, yet still with something of that far vision of what this land, and the outcome of his work in it, might be, he wrote the following lines:

Oft in the twilight of the wood,
I own'd that aw'd prophetic mood,
Which sees the future as a dream,
And life a shadow'd woodland stream

Till through the boughs I chanc'd to see
The heavenly orb's bright revelry,
And felt assured, however late,

That time would be my advocate,
And make my aims, despite my fear,
As stars from darkness come, appear.[70]

There was no need for despondency. Time, indeed, has proved to be John Galt's advocate.

Notes

PREFACE

1 The present-day Ontario.

2 "A Statistical Account of Upper Canada" by J. B. Galt, Esq., the first article in Vol. 29 of the magazine for October – December 1807 and January 1808. Galt at the time gave his initials as "J. B." to distinguish him from his father who was also called John Galt.

3 For these and Galt's other comments on the Gilkison link with Canada, see the *Autobiography*, I, pp. 97 – 98.

4 *The Financial Post,* August, 1953.

5 "The Other Side of John Galt" by A. McMillan, in *Scottish Art and Letters,* May/July, 1902, p. 98.

6 J. W. Aberdein, *John Galt,* London 1936, p. xv.

7 C. Karr, *The Canada Land Company: The Early Years. An Experiment in Colonization 1823 - 1843* (Ottawa: 1974), p. 42.

CHAPTER 1

1 The Scottish Covenanters were those who, in defense of Presbyterianism, bound themselves from 1557 to 1643 to oppose the efforts principally of the Stuart Kings, Charles I and Charles II, to impose the Episcopalian version of Protestantism on the Scottish church and people.

2 The title of the book was to be *The Banished Covenanters.* See the Galt Papers: Unpublished Manuscripts. Ontario Public Archives, Toronto.

3 The portrait is owned by Mrs. C. Smith of Winnipeg, whose late husband, Mr. H. G. H. Smith, Q.C., was a great-grandson of John Galt.

4 *Aut.,* I, pp. 4 and 2.

5 *Ibid.,* I, p. 8.

6 *Ibid.,* I, p. 98.

7 *Ibid.,* I, pp. 5 – 7.

8 *Ibid.,* I, pp. 16 – 17.

9 *Ibid.,* I, pp. 312, 313 – 314.

10 From *Fragmentary Memories of Bygone Days, Modes and Manners.* Printed for private circulation. By Robert Little. R. W. S. and Margaret Little. (London: 1913).

11 Pigott Ms. The Bodleian Library, Oxford.

12 *Recollections of Galt* (1841). Pigott Ms.

13 *Aut.,* I, p. 11.

14 *Recollections of Galt.* Pigott Ms.

15 T. W. Hamilton, F. S. I. *John Galt: The Man, His Life and Work* (Greenock: 1947), p. 5. Papers of the Greenock Philosophical Society.

16 A. F. McJannet, *Royal Burgh of Irvine* (Glasgow: 1938), p. 141.

17 Cf. what Galt says in the *Autobiography,* I, p. 11: "My progress during 1788 and 89 was not equal to my companions."

18 See McJannet, *op. cit.*

19 *Sir Andrew Wylie of that Ilk* (London: undated), p. 31.

20 Goatfell.

21 *Sir Andrew Wylie*, op. cit., p. 372.

22 "To the River Peneus." See *The Collected Poems of John Galt, 1779 - 1839*. Vol. I, 1969. Edited by H. B. Timothy, p. 366.

23 *Aut.*, I, p. 9.

24 *Ibid.*, I, p. 16.

25 *Ibid.*, I, p. 17.

26 The reference is probably to an equestrian statue of William of Orange which, until recent years, stood in the Trongate at Glasgow.

27 *Aut.*, I, p. 346.

28 John Galt Papers, Public Archives, Ottawa.

29 "Irvine Water. On seeing a Picture of a Favourite Scene of my Boyhood." *The Collected Poems of John Galt, 1779 - 1839, op. cit.*, p. 304.

CHAPTER 2

1,2 *Aut.*, I, p. 15.

3 Pigott Ms. The Bodleian Library, Oxford.

4 *Aut.*, I, pp. 19, 20 – 21.

5 G. D. Brown, *The House With The Green Shutters,* first published in 1901, reprinted by Collins, Glasgow and London (undated), p. 94.

6 *Recollections,* Pigott Ms.

7 *Ibid.*

8 See R. P. Gillies, *Memoirs of a Literary Veteran,* 1851, Vol. III, Ch. III.

9 *Aut.*, I, pp. 38 – 39.

10 *Ibid.*, I, pp. 40 – 42.

11 *Ibid.*, I, pp. 59 – 61.

12 *The Greenock News-Clout,* 1849. The portrait Galt passed on was accompanied by a poem written by him and published in the *News-Clout* with the title "Galt's First Love." See *The Collected Poems of John Galt, 1779 - 1839, op. cit.*, p. 325, and the Notes at the end of the volume.

13 Miss Elizabeth Henderson, a granddaughter of John Henderson, was living some years ago at Linlithgow in east central Scotland. In a letter she wrote to the late Professor G. H. Needler of Toronto occurs the statement: "My grandaunt, my grandfather's sister, was John Galt's first love. She died when she was about 19, at Plymouth or the Isle of Wight, where my grandfather had taken her for her health. We have two miniatures of her. One was in John Galt's possession, but he must have given it back when he married, or some time after she died . . . he would meet her in her home in Greenock."

14 See *The Collected Poems of John Galt, 1779-1839, op. cit.* The poem, set to music by Galt, is appended to the *Autobiography,* Vol. I.

15 *Aut.*, I, pp. 61 – 62.

16 *Ibid.*, I, pp. 115 – 116.

17 *Ibid.*, I, Second Epoch, Ch. III.

18 *Recollections.* Pigott Ms.

19 *Aut.*, I, pp. 113 – 114.

20 For what follows, to the end of the chapter, see *Aut.,* I, pp. 117 – 226 *passim.*

21 See letter of introduction and safe conduct issued to Galt by the Turkish authorities, November 27, 1810; addressed to Lieutenant Colonel Aga Receb, C. O. border troops. John Galt Papers. Public Archives, Ottawa.

22 The order Galt received to refrain from walking round the fortifications at Vidin recalls an earlier incident which occurred in his itinerary. He got off the ship conveying him up the Gulf of Smyrna

to take the measurements of "an enormous piece of brass ordinance" at one of the coastal batteries, in full view of the garrison.

CHAPTER 3

1 *Aut*, I, pp. 228 – 229.

2 Pigott Ms. The Bodleian Library, Oxford.

3 *Aut.*, I, p. 231.

4 An obvious allusion to the Buchanites. Their founder, Mrs. Buchan, gave out that she was the woman spoken of in the New Testament book of Revelation (ch. 12) and that the Relief Church minister in Irvine was "the man child whom she had brought forth." The Buchanites were anything but a large and flourishing sect. Neither John Galt nor anyone related to him ever belonged to it.

5 *The Literary Life and Miscellanies*, 3 vols. (London and Edinburgh: 1834), II, 36.

6 J. Ashton, *Social England Under the Regency*, New edition, illustr. (London: 1899), p. 317.

7 Pigott Ms., *op. cit.*

8 Aberdein, *op. cit.*, p. 80.

9 The portrait of Elizabeth Galt referred to is in the possession of Mr. and Mrs. T. B. Heney of Montreal. Mrs. Heney is a great-granddaughter of John Galt.

10 Pigott Ms., *op. cit.*

11 *Aut.*, I, pp. 258, 260 – 261.

12 See M. Sadleir, *The Strange Life of Lady Blessington,* Revised American edition (New York: 1947).

13 E. J. Lovell, Jr. *Lady Blessington's Conversations of Lord Byron,* Edited with an Introduction and Notes. (Princeton, N. J.: 1969), p. 147.

14 Pigott Ms., *op. cit.*

15 Galt's *George the Third, His Court and Family,* in two volumes, appeared in 1820. It was in honour of the royal family that Galt gave the name of Guelph to the first settlement he founded in Upper Canada.

16 See A. Morrison, *The Blessington Papers,* Second Series 1882 – 93. (London: 1895).

17 Reproduced in a paper on John Galt by Archibald Fullarton (who was distantly related to him) in *The Scottish American Journal,* New York, April 7, 1909.

18 John Galt Papers. Vol. I. Correspondence 1817 – 1839. Public Archives, Ottawa. Notices of Galt's appointment as agent for the claimants occur in the *Upper Canada Legislative Council Journals* 1821 – 24, p. 25, and in the *Upper Canada House of Assembly Journals* 1821 – 24, pp. 219 and 639.

19 There is nothing about Grant in the *Canadian Dictionary of National Biography.*

20 Colonial Office, 42.369.

21 *Aut.*, I, pp 278 – 279.

22 For the voluminous correspondence on the war claims see C. O. 42.380, 42.382, 42.387, 42.396 and 42.399.

CHAPTER 4

1 From Galt's description of his colonizing project in the *Autobiography* II, pp. 170 – 171.

2 *Aut.*, I, p. 280.

3 *Memoir* prefaced to the 1841 edition of Galt's *Annals of the Parish* and *The Ayrshire Legatees*.

4 *Two Note Books of Thomas Carlyle,* ed. C. E. Norton, (New York: 1898), p. 248.

5 McJannet, *op. cit.*, pp. 218 – 219.

6 *Recollections of Literary Characters and Celebrated Places* (London: 1854), Vol. II, Ch. V.

7 J. Prebble, *The Highland Clearances* (London: 1963), p. 148.

8 *Aut.*, I, p. 294.

9 February 16, 1824. Reproduced in the *Autobiography*, I, p. 299.

10 From Downing Street, London, April 23, 1824.

11 *The Cambridge History of the British Empire* (Cambridge: 1930), VI, pp. 252 – 253 and see *Report on the Affairs of British North America* by the Earl of Durham, 1812, ed. Lucas (Oxford: 1912), III, p. 52; II, p. 223.

12 See the Bathurst Papers, Loan 57/56, 1824. "Private" letters from various correspondents in North America. The British Library Manuscript Room, British Museum, London, England.

13 A. Wilson, *The Clergy Reserves of Upper Canada: A Canadian Mortmain* (Toronto: 1968), p. 105.

14 *Ibid.*, pp. 177 – 178.

15 The ease with which Galt could mix business and literature is illustrated by the "Letters from New York" which recall his travels from New York to Upper Canada as a member of the commission, and which, signed "A," he contributed in 1829 – 30 to the *New Monthly Magazine*.

16 *Aut.*, I, p. 319.

17 C. O. 42.375.

18 The alien question is discussed at length by G. M. Craig in his *Upper Canada: The Formative Years 1784 – 1841* (Toronto: 1963).

19 C. O. 42.381. Galt to Hillier, December 24, 1827.

20 *Aut.*, I, Epoch Fifth, Chapter IV.

Strachan also took part in the arrangement reached with Rolph.

21 *Ibid.*, I, p. 316.

22 From letter to his sister, dated at Eskgrove December 12, 1825. John Galt Papers. Public Archives, Ottawa.

23 From St. Helen's Place, London, August 30, 1825. Canada Company Records. Correspondence.

24 C. O. 42.379. Barrow to Horton, September 5, 1826; C. O. 42.406. Galt to Horton, September 6, 1826.

25 C. O. 42.406. Galt to Horton, May 13, 1826; C. O. 42.410. Galt to R. W. Hay, December 14, 1829; Hay to Galt, June 5, 1829 and December 17, 1829; Galt to Goderich, December 5, 1830; Horton to R. W. Hay, April 14, 1831, the original of which in the Catton Collection of Wilmot Horton Papers runs to fourteen foolscap pages.

26 Mistranslated by a Canadian professor of Classics "the soil does not change the man."

27 Canada Company Ledgers. Ontario Public Archives, Toronto. The ledger referred to also contains an application from Wilmot Horton "wishing to purchase the Crown Reserves in the little Peninsula of the Township of Murray in the Midland District at the current price at which Lands in similar situations are sold."

28 Dunlop graduated in medicine from the University of Glasgow; ran away from home to enlist in the British forces when his father remarried; and served in Canada in the war of 1812. During the war the Canadians, to counteract the naval operations of the Americans on the upper lakes, planned the construction of a large warship for which a new dockyard was to be created at

Penetanguishene thirty miles north of Lake Simcoe. The purpose of the road opened up under Dunlop's supervision was to establish communication between the dockyard and the lake.

29 "Instructions to the Warden of the Forests." Canada Company Records. September 11, 1826.

30 As communicated by Galt to Horton on September 26, 1826. Q series, 369. Public Archives, Ottawa.

31 September 4, 1826. C. O. 42.406.

32 From Musselburgh, September 28, 1826. Galt writing to Horton on August 25, 1826, reckoned that he would probably be away for eight months. C. O. 42.406.

33 February 16, 1826. C. O. 42.405.

34 *Aut.*, I, p. 355.

35 Q. 346,1. See also *Aut.*, I, p. 354.

36 *The Cambridge History of the British Empire* (Cambridge: 1930), V1, p. 260.

37 A. Dunham, *Political Unrest in Upper Canada 1815 -1836.* (London: 1927), p. 2.

38 "Upper Canada and the Conservative Tradition" in *Profiles of a Province. Studies in the history of Ontario,* Published by Ontario Historical Society, (Toronto: 1967), p.20.

39 G. M. Craig, *Upper Canada: The Formative Years 1784-1841* (Toronto: 1963), p. 1.

40 Dunham, *op. cit.,*p. 6.

41 *Ibid.,* p. 71.

42 *Ibid.,* p.3.

43 D. McLeod, *A Brief Review of the Settlement of Upper Canada* with a new introduction by William F. E. Morley, (Belleville, Ontario: 1972), p. 82.

44 Dunham, *op. cit.,* p.16.

45 W. S. Wallace, *The Family Compact,* Chronicles of Canada Series. (Toronto: 1915), p. 48.

46 *Report on the Affairs of British North America,* pp. 147 – 148.

47 *The Cambridge History of The British Empire,* V1, pp. 260 – 261.

48 *Ibid.,* V1, p. 262.

49 Portrait in the Department of Education at Toronto.

50 *The Cambridge History of the British Empire,* V1, p. 259.

51 McLeod, *op.cit.,* Ch. X1, *passim.*

52 A. Wilson, *The Clergy Reserves of Upper Canada: A Canadian Mortmain* (Toronto: 1968), p. 59.

53 Dunham, *op. cit.,* p. 103.

54 N. Macdonald, *Canada, 1763 - 1841, Immigration and Settlement. The Administration of the Imperial Land Regulations* (London, New York, Toronto: 1869), p. 369.

55 Dunham, *op. cit.,* p. 121.

56 *Ibid.,* p. 178.

57 Wilson, *op. cit.,* p. 62.

58 A. Ewart, and J. Jarvis, "The Personnel of the Family Compact, 1791 – 1841" in the *Canadian Historical Review,* Vol. 7, No. 3, Sept., 1926.

59 *The Cambridge History of the British Empire,* V1, p. 254.

60 *The Arthur Papers,* ed. C. R. Sanderson, (Toronto: 1957 – 59), II, p. 116.

61 Macdonald, *op. cit.,* pp. 367 – 368.

CHAPTER 5

1 Adapted from the first verse of "The Canadian Boat Song."

2 *Aut.,* II, p. 52.

3 Q Series, 346, 1. Public Archives, Ottawa.

4 *Aut.,* II, pp. 4 – 7. On December 24,

1827 Galt wrote to Hillier pointing out that he had explained to Maitland how he came to be in correspondence with Mackenzie and that Maitland did not seem to regard his explanation as unsatisfactory. He also provided Hillier with a résumé of what had passed between himself and Rolph and assured Hillier that he had ceased to have any dealings with the latter. C. O. 42.-381.

5 *Aut.,* II, p. 7.

6 Wilmot Horton Papers (Catton Collection in custody of the Derbyshire County Library).

7 The correspondence passing at this time between Galt and Maitland is reproduced in the *Autobiography,* II, pp. 8 – 30.

8 W. S. Wallace, *The Family Compact,* Chronicles of Canada Series (Toronto: 1915), p. 26.

9 Cf. Galt's letter to Horton of June 2, 1827. C. O. 42.408.

10 Q. 346, 1.

11 *Aut.,* II, p. 32, footnote.

12 *The Collected Poems of John Galt, 1779 – 1839.* Vol. I, 1969. Edited by H. B. Timothy, pp. 310 – 311.

13 *Aut.,* I, p. 334.

14, 15 See T. A. Talbot, *Five Years' Residence in the Canadas* (Toronto: 1824).

16 See H. Scadding, *Toronto of Old* (Toronto: 1878).

17 *Aut.,* II, p. 52.

18 Canada Company Records. Correspondence (drawn on from this point to the end of the chapter for Galt's dialogue with the Directors.)

19 Misc. Mss. 1827. Ontario Public Archives, somewhat paraphrased.

20 Galt's 'tide of emigration' may sound somewhat exaggerated; but, in a letter to a friend in Detroit on June 26, 1827, a Mr. G. McDougall mentioned that the operations of the Canada Company were beginning to be developed in that area under the superintendence of Galt and Dunlop and that preparations were being made for "ten thousand emigrants from England." In the Burton Historical Collection, Detroit Public Library.

21 See *Aut.,* II, pp. 56 – 60.

22 From Prior's report on developments at Guelph, dated October 1, 1827. Canada Company Records. Correspondence.

23 Simon McGillivray to Colonel Cockburn, October 16, 1824. Canada Company Records. Correspondence.

24 *Aut.,* II, p. 65.

25 C. O. 42.381; 42.382.

26 *Aut.,* II, pp. 65 –68. The letter accompanying the application sent to Hillier is reproduced in full at pp. 66 – 68 of the *Autobiography.*

27 *Aut.,* II, pp. 143, 149 – 150.

28 Galt to Maitland (private), September 26, 1827.

29 *Aut.,* II, pp. 61 –62.

30 *Ibid.,* II, pp. 103 – 104.

31 *Ibid.,* II, pp. 90 – 91, footnote.

32 *Ibid.,* II, p. 60.

33 *Ibid.,* II, p. 90, footnote.

34 *Ibid.,* II, p. 92.

35 From Musselburgh, March 17, 1827.

36 From Musselburgh, April 20, 1827.

37 From Musselburgh, June 30, 1827.

38 From Reading, September 17, 1827. Galt's wife moved from Musselburgh to Reading in August 1827, and put up there, as she wrote on August 25, in a small bed-sitting room in Reynold's lodging

house in Bridge Street, at a rent of £1 a week, so that Alex. might be able to attend Valpy's school as a day pupil with his brothers who were boarders.

CHAPTER 6

1 *Aut.*, II, pp. 70 – 71.

2 See R. and K. M. Lizars, *In the Days of the Canada Company* (Toronto: 1896), pp. 65 – 66.

3 Transcribed from the Survey Records of the Ontario Department of Lands and Forests, and annotated by R. M. Lewis; read at the annual meeting of the Ontario Historical Society on June 21, 1957; and published by permission of the Surveyor General.

4 The Nith is the river which flows through the town of Dumfries in the south of Scotland and enters the Solway Firth close to William Dickson's birthplace. The renaming of Smith's Creek may have been intended as a return compliment to Dickson for calling his village settlement after Galt.

5 See Lizars, *op. cit.*, p. 69.

6 C. O. 42.408.

7 *Aut.*, II, pp. 71 – 80, condensed.

8 See *Aut.*, I, Epoch Fourth, Ch. XI.

9 See *Aut.*, II, p. 80f.

10 J. MacTaggart, *Three Years in Canada*, 2 vols. (London: 1829), II, pp. 277 – 278.

11 C. O. 42.382. Galt to Hillier, July 23, 1827, thanking him for taking steps to determine the truth of the rumour, which, Galt mentioned, was fabricated by certain malicious individuals whom Burwell found it necessary to discharge after Dunlop's party reached Lake Huron. Galt's concern in the matter was for the effect the rumour might have, not only on the friends of members of the party, but also on the interests of the Canada Company.

12 *Aut.*, II, p . 122.

13 *Ibid.*, II, p. 121.

14 See "Reverend Proudfoot's Diary 1833," in *Huron Historical Notes,* Vol. II, 1966.

15 See "The Huron Road," in *Huron Historical Notes*, Vol. II, 1966.

16 C. O. 42.408.

17 *Ibid.*

18 V. Lauriston, "A Century of Goderich," in the *Canadian Geographical Journal*, Vol. V., No. 2, August, 1932.

19 Lizars, *op. cit.*, p. 236.

20 Mentioned in Proudfoot's diary.

21 *Ibid.*

22 See Lizars, *op. cit.*, p. 225.

23 Original in my possession.

24 *Aut.*, II, p. 140.

25 *Ibid.*, II, p. 89.

26 S. Strickland, *Twenty-seven Years in Canada West* (London: 1853), I, pp. 196 – 197.

27 John Howison, *Sketches of Upper Canada* (Edinburgh and London: 1821), pp. 192 – 193.

28 *Ibid.*, p. 194.

29 *Ibid.*, p. 267.

30 *Ibid.*, p. 234.

31 *Ibid.*, pp. 61 – 62.

32 *Ibid.*, pp. 225 – 226.

33 MacTaggart, *op. cit.*

34 Lauriston, *op. cit.*

CHAPTER 7

1 *Aut.*, II, p. 166.

2 *Ibid.*, II, p. 93.

3 See Sir E. Vaughan, "Scottish Settlers for Canada, from Venezuela: a bureaucratic problem in 1827" (awaiting publication), which, with Sir Edgar's permission,

has been drawn on pretty freely for the account given of the La Guayra emigrants in this chapter.

4 The arrangements referred to were never shown to have existed.

5 See C. C. James, "The Last of the La Guayrians (Wellington County, Ontario.)," in *Ontario Historical Society Papers and Records.* Toronto, 1917, XV; and J. J. Talman. "An Episode in Latin-American and Canadian Relations," in *Ontario Historical Society Papers and Records.* Toronto, 1946, XXVII.

6 *Aut.*, II, p. 104.

7 Lizars, *op: cit.*, p. 88.

8 *Aut.*, II, p. 105.

9 *Ibid.*, II, p. 108.

10 The family remained at Burlington Bay till the end of the summer when the boys were sent to school in Lower Canada (Quebec). Galt, as we learn from his letter of October 5, 1828 to Moir, moved with his wife early in September of that year to take up permanent residence in the renovated Priory at Guelph.

11 *Aut.*, II, p. 121.

12 *Ibid.*, II, p. 119.

13 *Ibid.*, II, p. 118.

14 The Dalhousie papers. Scottish Record Office. Edinburgh. This was not the first instance of Galt's casting about for another occupation. In a letter dated at Guelph, February 22, 1828, he submitted to Huskisson, and sent a copy to Lord Goderich of, an outline of a plan to assimilate the currency of the North American provinces with that of England. He expressed the hope that, if the plan were adopted, he might be appointed superintendent for, as he said, although his salary (£2,000) as manager for the Canada Company was satisfactory and although the duty was agreeable to his inclinations, circumstances with which Huskisson was acquainted had left him no desire to remain in the Company's service. C. O. 42.387.

15 *Aut.*, II, pp. 124 – 125, 127.

16 *Ibid.*, II, p. 127.

17 *Ibid.*, II, Epoch Seventh, Ch. VII.

18 *Ibid.*, II, p. 301 (Appendix).

19 *Ibid.*, II, p. 128.

20 *Ibid.*, II, pp. 159 – 160.

21 Strickland, *op. cit.*, pp. 201 – 202.

22 The eldest of the four children of Mrs. Galt's cousin in Glasgow (Mrs. Stevenson by her married name), who, at the death of their father toward the end of November 1828, were left unprovided for.

23 *Aut.*, II, p. 161.

CHAPTER 8

1 *Aut.*, II, pp. 161 – 163.

2 *Ibid.*, II, pp. 164 – 165.

3 *Ibid.*, II, p. 167.

4 See H. Dixon, *The London Prisons: With an account of the more distinguished persons who have been confined in them. To which is added, A Description of the Chief Provincial Prisons* (London: 1850).

5 *Aut.*, II, p. 170.

6 *The Cambridge History of the British Empire* (Cambridge: 1930). VI, p. 199.

7 *Aut.*, II, p. 312 (Appendix).

8 Canada Company Papers. Ontario Provincial Archives, Toronto.

9 *Ibid.*

10 William Jerdan in his *Men I Have Known* (London: 1866), describes Barn Cottage as "pretty old."

11 *Aut.*, II, p. 202.

12 See *Aut.*, II, Epoch Eighth, Ch. X.

13 C. O. 42.428. British American Land Company.

14 The Grey Papers. Department of Palaeography and Diplomatic. University of Durham, England.

15 See Galt's correspondence with Moir for April 1833 and March 1834.

16 From Dalhousie Castle, August 31, 1833.

17 John Galt Papers. Supplementary Correspondence 1806 – 1872. Public Archives, Ottawa.

18 From London, April 28, 1834. Burton Historical Collection. Detroit Public Library.

19 Letter from the King's private secretary. March 12, 1834.

20 See *Aut.*, I, pp. 25 – 26.

21 From Dalhousie Castle, July 31, 1834.

22 John Galt Papers. Vol. I. Correspondence 1817 – 1839. Public Archives, Ottawa.

23 From Greenock, November 18, 1834.

24 Sprig was its name, as we learn from verses addressed to it by Galt.

25 From an article on Galt by Archibald Fullarton in the April 7, 1909 issue of *The Scottish American Journal,* published at New York.

26 Gilmour's notes are among the Pigott papers in the Bodleian Library, Oxford.

27 My own.

28 C. O. 42.382.

29 A. Dunham, *Political Unrest in Upper Canada, 1815 – 1836* (London: 1927), pp. 113, 144-145.

30 W. S. Wallace, *The Family Compact* (Toronto: 1915) p. 4.

31 A. Wilson, *The Clergy Reserves of Upper Canada: A Canadian Mortmain.* (Toronto: 1968), p. 62.

32 C. O. 42.378. August 14, 1826.

33 Quotations from E. W. Spaulding, *His Excellency George Clinton: Critic of the Constitution,* 2nd edition. (Port Washington: 1964). See also W. McDonald, on George Clinton in the *American Historical Review,* October, 1938, XXXXIV, pp. 144 – 145.

34 In *Blackwood's Magazine,* No. XXVI for September 1829.

35 *Aut.,* II. p. 320 (Appendix).

36 C. O. 42.378. The letter is dated August 14, 1826 but the name of the recipient is not given.

37 *Aut.,* I, pp. 231 – 232.

38 Dunham, *op. cit.,* p. 126.

39 W. H. Graham, *The Tiger of Canada West* (Toronto: 1962), p. 44.

40 *Ibid.,* p. 70.

41 J. L. Morison, "John Galt as Colonist," in *The Glasgow Herald* "Scots in Canada" series, March 24, 1944.

42 C. Karr, "Social Unrest in the Huron Tract 1833 – 1843," *Western Ontario Historical Notes.* Vol. XXIV, No. 2. Fall 1968, p. 3.

43 L. J. Burpee, "A Family of Nation Builders; The Story of the Galts I John Galt, Colonizer and Super-Pioneer of Upper Canada," in *Saturday Night* for July 23, 1927, p. 2.

44 D. Carswell, "John Galt of the Canada Company. An Author Whose Genius Has Never Been Properly Recognized," in *The New Statesman* for December 20, 1930.

45,46 F. S. L. Ford, "William Dunlop 1792 – 1848" (paper read before the Academy of Medicine, Toronto, on Library and Historical Night, January 6, 1931; published in *The Canadian*

Medical Association Journal for August 1931 and issued in booklet form later the same year).

47 C. Karr, *The Canada Land Company: The Early Years. An Experiment in Colonization 1823 – 1843* (Ottawa: 1974), p. 50.

48 I. A. Gordon, *John Galt: The Life of a Writer.* (Edinburgh: 1972), p. 86.

49 Strickland, *Twenty-seven Years in Canada West* (London: 1853), I, p. 240.

50 See W. L. Mackenzie, *Sketches of Canada and the United States* (London: 1833).

51 Karr, *op. cit., loc. cit.*

52 *Aut.,* II, pp. 2 – 3 *passim.*

53 Burpee, *op. cit.*

54 Jerdan, *Men I Have Known, op. cit.*

55 Hamilton, *op. cit.,* p. 24.

56 *The Life and Times of Sir Alexander Tilloch Galt* (Toronto: 1920). pp. 28 – 29.

57 From "The Canada Company" (April 1836), quoted in the Misses Lizars' *In the Days of the Canada Company,* p. 129f.

58 Morison, *op. cit.*

59 See "The Speculawtor" which appeared in *Tait's Magazine* in 1838.

60 *Recollections of Literary Characters and Celebrated Places, op. cit.,* II, Ch. V.

61 Graham, *op. cit.,* p. 43.

62 R. K. Gordon, *John Galt* (Toronto: 1950), p. 54.

63 Aberdein, *op. cit.,* p. xvii.

64 *Eighty Years' Progress of British North America,* various contributors (Toronto: 1864), p. 32.

65 *Ibid.,* p. 40.

66 Burpee, *op. cit.*

67 *The Cambridge History of the British Empire,* V1, pp. 251 – 252.

68 See the Bathurst papers. Loan 57/18. British Library Manuscript Room. British Museum, London.

69 See G. W. Brown, *Building the Canadian Nation* (Toronto: 1942 – 1955), pp. 200 – 201; J. Howison, *Sketches of Upper Canada* (Edinburgh and London: 1821), p. 167; note on John Galt in the British Broadcasting Corporation's publication, *The Listener* for April 11, 1939, p. 42; Burpee, *op. cit.,* p. 2; report in the *Greenock Gazette* of a lecture entitled "John Galt in Canada," delivered to the Greenock Philosophical Society on the evening of October 20, 1933 by Professor J. L. Morison of Durham University.

70 *The Collected Poems of John Galt, 1779 – 1839,* Vol. I, 1969, edited by H. B. Timothy, p. 320.

Bibliography

Aberdein, J.W., *John Galt* (London:1936).
Ashton, J., *Social England Under the Regency* (London:1899).

Bathurst Papers, the: The British Library Manuscript Room, British Museum, London, England.
Blackwood's Edinburgh Magazine, No.XXVI for September, 1829.
Brown, G.D., *The House With The Green Shutters* (Glasgow and London:undated).
Brown, G.W., *Building the Canadian Nation* (Toronto: 1942–1955).
Burton Historical Collection, the; Detroit Public Library.

Cambridge History of the British Empire, The; (Cambridge:1930), vol. VI.
Canada Company Records. Ontario Public Archives, Toronto.
Canadian Dictionary of National Biography, The.
Canadian Geographical Journal, The; vol.V., No.2, August, 1932.
Craig, G.M., *Upper Canada : The Formative Years 1784–1841* (Toronto: 1963).

Dalhousie Papers, the; Scottish Record Office, Edinburgh.
Dixon, H., *The London Prisons : With an account of the more distinguished persons who have been confined in them. To which is added, A Description of the Chief Provincial Prisons* (London:1850).
Dunham, A., *Political Unrest in Upper Canada 1815-1836* (London: 1927).
Dunlop, A., *Dunlop of that Ilk, Memorabilia of the Families of Dunlop* (Glasgow: 1898).
Durham, the Earl of; *Report on the Affairs of British North America,* 1812, ed. Lucas (Oxford:1912).

Eighty Years' Progress of British North America (Toronto:1864).

Ford, F.S.L., *William Dunlop 1792-1848* (Toronto:1931).

Galt, H.S., *The Galt Families. Notes on their Origin and their History with Genealogical Lists* (Peiping:1938).
Galt, J., *The Life and Administration of Cardinal Wolsey* (London:1812).
Galt, J., *Voyages and Travels in the Years 1809, 1810, 1811* (London:1812).
Galt, J., *Letters from the Levant* (London:1813).
Galt, J., ed. *The New British Theatre* in four vols. (London 1814–15).
Galt, J., *George the Third, his Court and Family* in two vols. (London:1820).

165

Galt, J., *Annals of the Parish; or the Chronicles of Dalmailing* (Edinburgh and London:1821).

Galt, J., *The Ayrshire Legatees* (Edinburgh:1821).

Galt, J., *The Provost* (Edinburgh and London:1822).

Galt, J., *The Entail; or the Lairds of Grippy* in three vols. (Edinburgh:1823).

Galt, J., *Lawrie Todd; or the Settlers in the Wood* in three vols. (London:1830).

Galt, J., *Life of Lord Byron* (London:1830).

Galt, J., *Bogle Corbet; or the Emigrants* in three vols. (London:1831).

Galt, J., *The Autobiography* in two vols. (London:1833).

Galt, J., *Eben Erskine* in three vols. (London:1833).

Galt, J., *The Literary Life and Miscellanies* in three vols. (London and Edinburgh:1834).

Galt, J., *Sir Andrew Wylie of that Ilk* (London:undated).

Galt, J., *Ringan Gilhaize; or, the Times of the Covenanters* (Glasgow:undated).

Galt Papers, the; Unpublished Manuscripts, Ontario Public Archives, Toronto.

Gillies, R.P., *Memoirs of a Literary Veteran*. 1851

Gordon, I.A., *John Galt : The Life of a Writer* (Edinburgh: 1972).

Gordon, R.K., *John Galt* (Toronto:1950).

Graham, W.H., *The Tiger of Canada West* (Toronto:1962).

Grey Papers, the; Department of Palaeography and Diplomatic, University of Durham, Durham, England.

Hamilton, T.W., *John Galt : The Man, His Life and Work* (Greenock:1947).

Howison, J., *Sketches of Upper Canada* (Edinburgh and London: 1821).

Huron Historical Notes. Huron County Historical Society.

Jerdan, W., *Men I Have Known* (London:1866).

John Galt Papers, the; Public Archives, Ottawa.

Karr, C., *The Canada Land Company : The Early Years, An Experiment in Colonization* 1823-1843 (Ottawa:1974).

Lewis, R.M., *The Diary of Mahlon Burwell, transcribed and annotated* (Toronto:1975).

Little, R. and M., *Fragmentary Memories of Bygone Days, Modes and Manners* (London:1913).

Lizars, R. and K.M., *In the Days of the Canada Company* (Toronto:1896).

Lovell, E. J., Jr., *Lady Blessington's Conversations of Lord Byron* (Princeton, N.J.:1969).

Lumsden, H., *The Bibliography of John Galt* (Glasgow:1931).

Macdonald, N., *Canada, 1763–1841: Immigration and Settlement. The Administration of the Imperial Land Regulations* (London, New York, Toronto:1869).

Mackenzie, W.L., *Sketches of Canada and the United States* (London:1833).

MacTaggart, J., *Three Years in Canada* in two vols. (London:1829).

McJannet, A.F., *Royal Burgh of Irvine* (Glasgow:1938).

McLeod, D., *A Brief Review of the Settlement of Upper Canada* (Belleville, Ontario:1972).

Moir, D.M., *Memoir of John Galt.* 1841.

Morrison, A., *The Blessington Papers* (London:1895).

Norton, C.E., ed. *Two Note Books of Thomas Carlyle* (New York:1898).

Ontario Historical Society Papers and Records.

Private correspondence, family papers, photographs, original documents etc., donated by certain of John Galt's present-day descendants, mainly in Canada.

Personal manuscripts, notes etc. on John Galt gifted by the late W. Brownlie Hendry, Bridge of Weir, Renfrewshire, Scotland.

Pigott Ms. and Papers. The Bodleian Library, Oxford.

Prebble, J., *The Highland Clearances* (London:1963).

Profiles of a Province. Studies in the History of Ontario , ed. Edith G. Firth (Toronto:1967).

Sadleir, M., *The Strange Life of Lady Blessington* (New York 1947).

Scadding, H., *Toronto of Old* in two vols. (Toronto:1878).

Series Q. Public Archives, Ottawa.

Skelton, O.D., *The Life and Times of Sir Alexander Tilloch Galt* (Toronto:1920).

Spaulding, E.W., *His Excellency George Clinton: Critic of the Constitution* (Port Washington:1964).

State Papers for Upper Canada, Series C.O. Record Office, London, England.

Strickland, S., *Twenty-seven Years in Canada West* in two vols. (London:1853).

Talbot, T.A., *Five Years' Residence in the Canadas* (Toronto:1824).

Thomson, K., *Recollections of Literary Characters and Celebrated Places* (London:1854).

Timothy, H.B., ed. *Collected Poems of John Galt, 1779–1839, The.* Vol.1 1969.

Upper Canada House of Assembly Journals for 1821–1824. Public Archives, Ottawa.

Upper Canada Legislative Council Journals for 1821–1824. Public Archives. Ottawa.

Wallace, W.S., *The Family Compact* (Toronto:1915).

Western Ontario Historical Notes. Lawson Memorial Library, The University of Western Ontario, London, Ontario.

Wilkie, J., *Historic Musselburgh* (Edinburgh and London:1919).

Wilmot Horton Papers (Catton Collection), the; Derbyshire Public Library, Derby, England.

Wilson, A., *The Clergy Reserves of Upper Canada : A Canadian Mortmain* (Toronto:1968).

Index